UP FOR THE CHALLENGE?

UP FOR THE CHALLENGE?

TAKE ON OVER **60** OF THE WORLD'S MOST
GRUELING AND SPECTACULAR SPORTS EVENTS

DOMINIC BLISS

TO MAUREEN AND GORDON BLISS. REMEMBER WHAT CHARLES DICKENS WROTE: "THE MEN WHO LEARN ENDURANCE ARE THEY WHO CALL THE WHOLE WORLD BROTHER."

PUBLISHED IN 2015 BY DOG 'N' BONE BOOKS
AN IMPRINT OF RYLAND PETERS & SMALL LTD
20–21 JOCKEY'S FIELDS   341 E 116TH ST
LONDON WC1R 4BW   NEW YORK, NY 10029

WWW.RYLANDPETERS.COM

10 9 8 7 6 5 4 3 2 1

TEXT © DOMINIC BLISS 2015
DESIGN AND PHOTOGRAPHY © DOG 'N' BONE BOOKS 2015

A CIP catalog record for this book is available from the Library of Congress and the British Library.

ISBN: 978 1 909313 75 0

Printed in China

Editor: Emma Hill
Designer: Eoghan O'Brien
Photography: See page 144 for credits

Follow Dominic Bliss on Twitter @DominicBliss

CONTENTS

PREPARE TO SUFFER

The sports races and challenges you'll see over the following pages, featured in all their body- and spirit-sapping glory, all share one thing in common: they push you to your absolute physical and mental limits.

Are they all spectacular? Without a doubt. Are they all grueling? Yes, but in very different ways.

Most of the endurance races—whether they feature cycling, running, swimming, horse-riding, paddling, hiking, skating, skiing, or sledding—require immense fitness, certain techniques, and lots of mental discipline.

But even the races that use motorized vehicles or wind power are monumentally testing, too. Driving a rickshaw the entire length of India, for example, or playing 18 holes of golf spread across nearly 850 miles (1,350 km) of the Australian outback may not require aerobic fitness, but they definitely call for staying power.

What is it about endurance sport that is so popular right now? Across the western world, as gym membership wanes, and team sports suffer, the likes of long-distance running, biking, and swimming (and often all three combined) are growing meteorically.

Ease of access helps. Anyone with just a modicum of fitness knows how to run, cycle, or swim. And with no teams

involved, busy people can easily organize their training. Outdoor sport appeals to people who spend their working lives confined inside office buildings—especially if you can access the countryside.

But none of this explains why a sane person would attempt (and pay) to run 500 miles (800 km) across a desert, or cycle over an entire mountain range, or cross-country ski in the polar regions. Perhaps standard-length races just don't cut the mustard any more. Why run 26.2 miles (42 km), or swim 20 lengths of your local pool when you can run 150 miles (240 km) and swim the length of an entire river?

But I believe there's one reason, more than any other, that we want to push ourselves to our physical and mental limits: because we're mollycoddled. In the western world, at least, with our safe homes and well-paid jobs, we rarely put ourselves outside of our comfort zones. Few of us have ever faced military conscription. Even fewer know what it's like to fight in a war.

Our wars are very different from those of our forefathers. Our battles involve running hundreds of miles across the Sahara Desert. Or cycling the entire USA. Or swimming the English Channel, and back again. Or rowing the Atlantic Ocean. Or sailing round the planet.

No bullets, no bombs. Just an uncomfortably large amount of mud, sweat, and tears.

CHAPTER 1

NORTH AMERICA

PIKES PEAK MARATHON

DISCIPLINE:
MOUNTAIN RUNNING

LOCATION:
MANITOU SPRINGS, COLORADO, USA

TOUGHNESS FACTOR:
✖ ✖ ✖ ✖ ✖ ✖ ✖ ✖ ✖ ✖

POTENTIAL HAZARDS:
LIGHTNING, THUNDERSTORMS, BROKEN LIMBS

WWW.PIKESPEAKMARATHON.ORG

If it's elevation you're after, then Pikes Peak Marathon in the Colorado Rockies will certainly deliver. Starting from Manitou Springs, at 6,299 ft (1,920 m) above sea level, the often narrow, winding, and rocky course rises steeply to 14,110 ft (4,300 m) at an average gradient of 11 percent. Once at the summit, runners turn around and head straight back down the mountain the way they came to complete the 26-mile (42-km) course. (There is also a half-distance option called the Pikes Peak Ascent.)

ABOVE: Pikes Peak runners often face thunderstorms when they've ascended the mountain. In 2005 a lightning strike knocked two athletes off their feet

Runners are exposed to all the elements the Rocky Mountains decide to throw at them, especially once they rise above the treeline. Heavy rain, strong winds, hail, sleet—even snow—should be expected. And this is midsummer! As well as dehydration and exposure (temperatures can vary by as much as 86°F (30°C) between the bottom and the top), severe thunderstorms threaten unwary competitors. "In 2004, we had six to eight inches of new snow on the peak," the organizers explain. "In 2005, hundreds of runners were stranded on the summit when a huge storm hit the mountain. Every day on Pikes Peak can bring rapid, frequent, and extreme weather changes." But worst of all is the lightning. "Mother Nature is very unpredictable regarding this element," says the race president, Ron Ilgen. "In 2005, a lightning strike between two runners knocked both of them over. One suffered first-degree burns on her shin; the rubber on her running shoes had actually melted in places."

With so many tree roots and rocks along the trail, runners often stumble and fall over. "Scrapes and cuts requiring stitches are common," Ilgen adds. "Falls can result in concussions, broken ribs and arms. In 2006, a woman fell on the descent, just below the timberline. The search and rescue team placed her arm in a splint and she proceeded down the course with eight miles remaining." Stoical to the end, she finished the race just 40 seconds before the cut-off time. "The finish-line medical area resembles a hospital emergency room," continues Ilgen, "with runners treated for dehydration and cuts. Some are actually sutured by the medical team. The more severe cases are transported to the hospital for treatment of broken bones and possible internal injuries." He remembers one year waving off a female runner as she and her broken ankle headed off in an ambulance. It turns out the break had occurred 10 miles (16 km) before the finish, yet she had soldiered on without alerting staff to her injury because she knew they would withdraw her from the race.

To add to the drama, bears and mountain lions are occasionally sighted on the course. None have yet felt the need to join in the chase, but stragglers are always told to remain wary.

ABOVE: Pikes Peak rises to 14,110 ft (4,300 m)

ABOVE : The steep terrain means some runners suffer concussions, broken ribs, arms, and ankles

BADWATER 135

DISCIPLINE:
RUNNING

LOCATION:
BADWATER, CALIFORNIA, USA

TOUGHNESS FACTOR:
✖✖✖✖✖✖✖✖✖

POTENTIAL HAZARDS:
HEAT EXHAUSTION, DEHYDRATION, MOUNTAIN LIONS

WWW.BADWATER.COM

"My brain was on fire. My body was burning up. Death Valley had laid me out flat, and now it was cooking me. My crew was telling me to get up, that they knew I could go on, but I could barely hear them. I was too busy puking, then watching the stream of liquid evaporate in the circle of light from my headlamp almost as fast as it splashed down on the steaming pavement. It was an hour before midnight, 105 incinerating, soul-sucking degrees."

This was Scott Jurek, one of the world's greatest ultrarunners, describing his 2005 experience of the Badwater 135 race in his biography **Eat & Run**. It's one of America's most infamous ultramarathons—staged in midsummer, 135 miles (217 km) long, and much of it uphill. "The world's toughest foot race" is its claim. The race route traverses Death Valley—site of the hottest atmospheric temperature ever recorded on planet Earth (134°F/57°C)—and extends most of the way up Mount Whitney, the highest summit in the contiguous United States. Unbelievably, despite the intense heat, no one has died while competing in the race, although plenty of runners have seen their shoes melt on the ferociously hot asphalt sections.

Anyone bold enough to enter the Badwater 135 is left under no illusion as to the physical and psychological demands of their task. "Heat illness and heat stroke are serious risks," the organizers warn. "These can cause death, renal shutdown, and brain damage. Runners may well require dozens of gallons of fluid during this race. The high altitude plus exertion can also produce various degrees of altitude sickness. This can lead to severe lung and brain swelling, and even death. Blisters are also a problem on this course, with pavement temperatures perhaps reaching 200 degrees."

There are no aid stations along the route so it's every man and woman for themselves. As Scott Jurek discovered in 2005.

But it wasn't the physical torture that knocked him sideways, it was the mental anguish. (As one competitor once explained: "The first half of the Badwater is run with the legs, the second half with the heart.") Scott had taken every precaution against the intense heat, wearing heat-reflective clothing, using an industrial sprayer to hose himself down, and consuming 60 fl oz (1.8 liters) of water every hour for the first six hours of the race. But still, 70 miles (112 km) into the race, he felt like he wanted to die.

After much soul searching, and vomiting, Scott eventually pulled himself together, continued running and won the entire race, setting a new course record of 24 hours and 36 minutes.

IRONMAN

Thanks to a history dating back to the late 1970s, and some brilliant marketing, the Ironman triathlon series is arguably the most famous in the world. Consisting of a 2.4-mile (3.9-km) swim, a 112-mile (180-km) bike ride and a standard-distance marathon, the races have gradually spread all over the globe so that now there are 40 events across six continents, culminating in Hawaii's annual Ironman Championship. There is also an enormously popular series of half-distance Ironman triathlons, known as Ironman 70.3, with around 80 races staged globally.

DISCIPLINE:
SWIMMING, CYCLING, RUNNING

LOCATION:
ORIGINALLY FROM HAWAII, NOW EVENTS ARE WORLDWIDE

TOUGHNESS FACTOR:
✗ ✗ ✗ ✗ ✗ ✗ ✗ ✗ ✗

POTENTIAL HAZARDS:
DEHYDRATION, HYPONATREMIA

WWW.IRONMAN.COM

The race was first set up to settle an argument over which athletes were fittest— swimmers, cyclists, or runners. US Navy officer John Collins suggested combining the Honolulu Marathon, the Waikiki Roughwater Swim, and the Around Oahu Bike Race into one grueling event. Written in the instruction booklet for the first race in 1978 was the following advice: "Swim 2.4 miles! Bike 112 miles! Run 26.2 miles! Brag for the rest of your life!" It has since become the event's mantra.

"In the world of triathlons, the iron distance creeps up on an athlete and becomes an all-consuming, passionate fixation," writes Davida Ander in **Outdoor Fitness** magazine. "It evolves into a do-or-die obligation, with a dedication that most onlookers would label manic. Some compare the final event to giving birth; others cannot describe the rush of emotions that encapsulates them during their voyage of 140 miles."

ABOVE: The cycling leg of the Ironman covers a similar length to an average stage of the Tour de France, but riders don't have the luxury of a team to help them to the finish.

ATHENS TO ATLANTA ROAD SKATE

It's America's oldest road-skating competition. The Athens to Atlanta Road Skate, which has been rolling since 1982, is an 87-mile (140-km) race across the US state of Georgia, mainly on country lanes.

DISCIPLINE:
**ROLLER SKATING
OR INLINE SKATING**

LOCATION:
ATHENS TO ATLANTA, GEORGIA, USA

TOUGHNESS FACTOR:
✖ ✖ ✖ ✖ ✖ ✖ ✖ ✖ ✖ ✖

POTENTIAL HAZARDS:
ROAD RASH, CAR COLLISION

WWW.A2A.NET

While the majority of competitors take it lightly (and there are shorter race distances on offer), a hardcore elite of skaters push themselves to their athletic limit. With that in mind, there are certain strict rules: "There will be zero tolerance of abusive, assaultive, bullying, intimidating, and/or verbally assaultive behavior of any kind, including foul language, striking another skater, pulling, pushing, blocking, and/or shoving," the organizers warn. Drafting behind motor vehicles or bicycles is also strictly forbidden.

In the early days, on roller skates, the winners took well over six hours. Modern winners—using the faster inline skates—complete the race in under five hours. One famous downhill section, called Silver Hill, sees them approaching 50 mph (80 km/h).

Eddy Matzger is a multiple winner of the Athens to Atlanta, and a bit of a legend in the event. He's also a legend in the world of inline skating in general. Not much is off-limits to Eddy and his skates: he's the first person to climb Mount Kilimanjaro, and the Great Pyramid of Giza, on skates (albeit off-road ones with inflatable tires). He has also skated his way through the Running of the Bulls in Pamplona. "Fast Eddy," they call him.

ABOVE: One section of the A2A sees skaters reaching speeds of 50 mph (80 km/h)

CATALINA CHANNEL SWIM

DISCIPLINE:
OCEAN SWIMMING

LOCATION:
**CATALINA CHANNEL,
CALIFORNIA, USA**

TOUGHNESS FACTOR:
✗✗✗✗✗✗✗✗ ✗ ✗

POTENTIAL HAZARDS:
**STRONG CURRENTS, DROWNING,
SHARK ATTACK, JELLYFISH
STINGS, KELP**

WWW.SWIMCATALINA.COM

It all started with the Wrigley Ocean Marathon back in 1927. Chewing-gum magnate William Wrigley Jr staged the race across the 20-mile (32-km) Catalina Channel (between Catalina Island and the California mainland) to promote the tourist resort he'd built on the island. With the then princely sum of US$25,000 in prize money for the winner, plenty of swimmers were keen to take part.

On race day 102 of them—some slathered in grease and nothing else—lined up on the start line at Catalina's Isthmus Cove. It was January, though, and the water was cold. So cold that five and a half hours later only 30 swimmers remained in the water. Ahead of the pack was young Canadian swimming champion George Young, who had hitchhiked much of the way to California to compete in the race. Young was cruising well ahead of all his rivals and looking strong until at 11p.m., just under 12 hours into the ordeal, he got tangled in a thick bed of kelp. He was just about to abandon when a tugboat pulled alongside with a telegram from his mother. She had been listening to her son's progress on the radio and wanted to give him extra encouragement. The tactic

33° 23' 16.39" N, 118° 24' 58.72" W

worked and Young pressed on, finally reaching the mainland at just after 3a.m., 15 hours and 44 minutes after he'd started. He was the only swimmer to complete the race.

"With his emergence from the water, a flare was shot to signify his finish," writes Penny Dean, author of **A History of the Catalina Channel Swims Since 1927** and current record holder for the swim. "It was estimated that 15,000 spectators were on hand for the finish. Bedlam broke loose afloat and ashore. Boat whistles, auto horns, and human throats joined in a chorus, flares of Roman fire lit the scene and its background of rocks." In the joy of victory, Young forgot that he'd removed his chafing swimsuit shortly after starting the swim and had completed the race naked. "I forgot that grease and graphite were my only covering as I rose out of the water at the shore, so I beat it back into the waves to my convoy boat," he later recalled.

Nowadays, thanks to much more comfortable swimsuits, Catalina Channel swimmers tend to remain clothed. Yet they still have to combat cold waters, seasickness (because of the enormous swells), and occasionally the unwanted attention of sharks and jellyfish. At the time of writing, more than 320 men and women have completed the marathon. Penny Dean's record time (set in 1976) is seven hours, 15 minutes, and 55 seconds.

OCEAN'S SEVEN

DISCIPLINE:
OCEAN SWIMMING

LOCATION:
GLOBAL

TOUGHNESS FACTOR:
✘✘✘✘✘✘✘✘

POTENTIAL HAZARDS:
DROWNING, HYPOTHERMIA, BAD WEATHER, MENTAL FATIGUE, AGGRESSIVE OCEAN-DWELLING ANIMALS

WWW.COOKSTRAITSWIM.ORG.NZ
WWW.KAIWICHANNELASSOCIATION.COM
WWW.TSUGARUCHANNELSWIMMING.COM
WWW.SWIM2AFRICA.COM

The Catalina, Irish (page 58), and English Channels (page 54) are three of a group of mighty swimming challenges known as Ocean's Seven. Comprising the rest of the group are Cook Strait (16 miles/26 km between the North and South Islands of New Zealand), the Kaiwi Channel (27 miles/43 km between Hawaii's Oahu and Molokai Islands), the Tsugaru Strait (12 miles/19 km between Honshu and Hokkaido in Japan), and the Strait of Gibraltar (8 miles/13 km between Portugal and Morocco).

At the time of writing, only seven people have completed all seven swims. Irishman Stephen Redmond was the first. "A real test of the head and the body," he said before his seventh and final swim, the Tsugaru Strait. Despite several abandoned attempts due to bad weather and rough seas, Redmond crossed the Japanese stretch of water in July 2012. On the flight back to Ireland he said he cried the entire journey before receiving a hero's welcome. "When swimming I think about my wife, my kids, I think about everybody—guys that are gone, people that are dead. It's a real hallucinating thing, swimming. The stupidest things come into your head and all that gets you through."

THE IDITAROD

DISCIPLINE:
SLED-DOG RACING

LOCATION:
ANCHORAGE TO NOME, ALASKA, USA

TOUGHNESS FACTOR:
✗✗✗✗✗✗✗✗ ✗ ✗

POTENTIAL HAZARDS:
BLIZZARDS, GALES, FREEZING CONDITIONS, ANGRY MOOSE

WWW.IDITAROD.COM

No one says "Mush!" any more. That's for amateurs. But you can still call sled-dog racers "mushers." And when it comes to the Iditarod, these are without doubt the most accomplished mushers in the world. The Iditarod Trail Sled-Dog Race, to use its full name, is a brutal long-distance race across the snowy wastes of Alaska.

THE IDITAROD IS A BRUTAL LONG-DISTANCE RACE

Staged every March, it sees mushers and their teams of—on average—16 dogs racing over 1,000 miles (1,600 km) between Alaska's biggest city Anchorage and Nome, a town on the edge of the Bering Sea, following the route of a traditional winter sled-dog supply trail. In even years competitors have to head south to north; in odd years north to south. It has been going since 1973 when just 33 mushers took part, and only 22 finished. Today there are normally around 50 competitors brave enough to set out into the freezing cold conditions with just a sled and a pack of huskies for company.

At the time of writing, the record for the race (eight days, 13 hours and four minutes) is held by Dallas Seavey, now star of National Geographic Channel's series **Ultimate Survival Alaska**. Seavey and his rivals must face a whole gamut of cold-weather hazards ranging from blizzards and gale-force winds to complete whiteouts and wind chills as low as -100°F (-70°C). One year an angry moose charged at Seavey. "When moose have no more body fat, they start metabolizing their muscles, and it creates a chemical imbalance," explains Seavey, who was forced to dispatch the huge mammal with his .357 Magnum.

Mushers have their supplies (human food, dog food, dog booties, headlamps, batteries, tools, and sled parts) flown ahead to each checkpoint. They choose where and when to rest, although there are three mandatory layovers. The most exciting stage of the race is normally the last dash to the finish when the leading teams are often within a few hours of one another. The 1978 race was the closest in Iditarod history when the winner, Dick Mackey, finished just a second ahead of runner-up Rick Swenson. Swenson's body may have crossed the finish line first, but Mackey was deemed champion since his leading dog's nose was just ahead of the rival pack. "As soon as I knew that my dogs had crossed the finish line before his, I went to flop into my sled, and I missed it and fell on the ground," Mackey later told **Alaska Dispatch News**. "And of course everybody thought I'd had a heart attack." Not that Swenson didn't enjoy victories of his own. He had already won the Iditarod the year before, and went on to win it again in 1979, 1981, 1982, and 1991, amassing a record five victories in all. They still call him "King of the Iditarod."

Of course, the most impressive athletes in the Iditarod are the dogs rather than the humans. Mostly mixed-breed huskies, bred for their endurance, tough feet, and mental attitude, they burn around 5,000 calories a day during the Iditarod. When you take into account their bodyweight, this equates to three-and-half-times the calorie burn of a Tour de France cyclist. Dogs have been known to die during this race.

YUKON ARCTIC ULTRA

DISCIPLINE:
**MOUNTAIN BIKING,
CROSS-COUNTRY SKIING,
OR RUNNING**

LOCATION:
**WHITEHORSE TO DAWSON CITY,
YUKON, CANADA**

TOUGHNESS FACTOR:
✖✖✖✖✖✖✖✖✖✖

POTENTIAL HAZARDS:
**HYPOTHERMIA, FROSTBITE,
HALLUCINATIONS**

WWW.ARCTICULTRA.DE

Mountain biking, cross-country skiing, or running...take your pick. Just be ready for serious snow, serious ice, and serious cold weather. Although there are several distances on offer, it's the 430-mile (692-km) race along part of the Yukon Quest Trail from Whitehorse to Dawson City (both towns in the Canadian territory Yukon) that is the daddy of them all.

LEFT: Most athletes choose to tackle the trail on foot and an average of one in three racers fail to reach the finish line

This takes place every two years. As well as all the usual cold-weather gear you'd expect, the long-distance competitors must also carry with them a GPS, crampons, a saw, and an avalanche shovel. A satellite phone is highly recommended.

Competitors are lucky if they snatch a few hours' sleep here and there in their bivouacs on the edge of the trail.

British runner Sean Brown completed the race in 2007, in a total time of 192 hours. (This was the 300-mile/482-km, not the full 430-mile/692-km route.) On the way he suffered serious shin splints, diarrhea (brought on by painkillers swallowed to alleviate the shin splints), and sleep deprivation. With temperatures dropping at times to -40°F (-40°C), he also felt more than a little chilly. "The cold monster wants your fingers, nose, and toes and isn't happy unless they're constantly going numb," he wrote in his blog. "The cold monster also tries to numb your brain, getting you to think and act slower and more irrationally." Brown discovered that, even with the best gloves money could buy, the ends of his fingers suffered bitterly.

The other monster was the sleep monster. "You can try various things to stave it off," he added. "Coffee, playing your ipod very loudly with inspiring music, talking to yourself, hallucinating—it doesn't really matter. It will get you and force you to [sleep in your bivouac] regardless of where you are and the temperature." At one point Brown's spectacles started to freeze, so he replaced them with ski goggles. But eventually these got so cold that they cracked right down the middle of the lens.

It wasn't all doom and gloom, though. At one point Brown found himself bathed in the ethereal green glow of the Northern Lights. "I was crossing lakes which were very big and quite beautiful. The aurora borealis had also come out and this part of the trail was undoubtedly the most beautiful and remote. A few times during the night I turned off my light and just marveled at where I was, halfway across a lake, a million miles from anywhere."

ABOVE: Mountain bikes must be equipped with extra-wide tyres in order to cope with the snow and icy conditions.

THE TEVIS CUP

DISCIPLINE:
**HORSE RIDING
AND TRAIL RUNNING**

LOCATION:
**LAKE TAHOE TO AUBURN,
CALIFORNIA, USA**

TOUGHNESS FACTOR:
✘ ✘ ✘ ✘ ✘

POTENTIAL HAZARDS:
FALL FROM HORSE

WWW.TEVISCUP.ORG

The sport of endurance riding sees two finely honed athletes—one human and one equine—racing long-distance across rough, often mountainous terrain. And the race that most consider the apogee of endurance riding is the Tevis Cup, a 100-mile (160-km) ordeal across the Rocky Mountains of California, following a particularly rugged section of an ancient Native American route called the Western States Trail.

To get an idea of just how rugged, check out some of the place names riders pass through: Cougar Rock, Last Chance, Devil's Thumb, Volcano Creek, No Hands Bridge, Black Hole of Calcutta. The elevation is harsh, too, starting at 7,220 ft (2,200 m) above sea level and dropping to just 705 ft (215 m) at its lowest point, with temperatures ranging from below freezing to well over 104°F (40°C).

Over the years some horses have perished, falling off cliffs along the way. So far no riders have lost their lives, although they occasionally cross the finishing line nursing broken bones. Organizers describe the race as "challenging, technical, and relentlessly demanding," boasting that **Time** magazine hadn't ranked it in the top 10 toughest endurance events in the world "for being a stroll in the park."

One of the greatest Tevis Cup heroes of all is Californian Jeremy Reynolds, winner in 2004, 2007, and 2011. Like all race participants, Reynolds and his faithful steed (he's twice won on CV Eli but most recently it was with Riverwatch) are subject to strict medical controls during competition. Support crews ensure both rider and mount are fully fed, watered, and cooled off. Each horse stops regularly for a medical by a vet, who checks for injuries or signs of over-riding. Any reason for concern and the horse and its rider are disqualified. For this reason, riders who learn to pace their steeds correctly, and understand equine physiology, often win races.

It was equine physiology that caused Reynolds to come unstuck in the 2012 edition of the Tevis Cup. Riding an Arabian mare called Cleopatrah, he was forced to pull out of the race when she "spooked along the trail and got injured, requiring a few stitches." The eventual winner that year was one Garrett Ford, achieving the quickest time on an Arabian gelding called The Fury.

Arabians are by far the most dominant breed when it comes to endurance riding. Since the Tevis Cup was first held in 1955, all but two of the winners have been Arabians or part-Arabians. "They don't get tired like other breeds," Reynolds explains. "There are some other breeds with a bit more speed, but they won't have the longevity."

Both Reynolds and his horses have longevity in spades. Many of his animals are former flat racers, trained for several seasons before entering long-distance competitions. And Reynolds is something of an athlete himself. A fairly accomplished ultradistance runner, he has competed in 50-mile (80-km) and 100-mile (160-km) foot races and knows exactly at which points to dismount during the Tevis Cup to run alongside his horse. "It's a real benefit if I can give the horse a break," he explains. While dismounted, he may travel at a slower pace than his mounted competitors, but by resting his horse on some of the more strenuous sections he gains more ground over his rivals in the long run.

One section of the Tevis Cup involves a very hot and very steep climb up through a canyon. Reynolds always dismounts at the bottom, choosing to speed hike alongside his horse. "At the bottom I quickly get passed by other riders," he says. "But by the time I reach the top of the canyon I've then passed whoever passed me because their horse is by then so tired and has to walk so slow." On his first Tevis Cup win, in 2004, he estimates that he ran or speed-hiked alongside his horse for about a quarter of the entire race.

Reynolds' fitness in the saddle gives him an advantage, too. "I think I have an upper hand because some people get tired from endurance riding and I don't at all. It really helps the horse if you can be an active rider, staying balanced and not slouching from being tired." This is, after all, a team sport. During competition Reynolds constantly reassures his horse, patting it, hugging it, and whispering encouragement. The relationship and trust between the two team members is crucial for riders in order to reach the finish. One of the Tevis Cup organizers explains: "For many riders, the miles traveled after sundown are the highlight of the ride. The temperatures have cooled and the horses seem to be reinvigorated as they move closer to the finish. People aren't talking much, and the sounds of the river can be heard below. Some riders find it to be a very spiritual experience."

TOUR DIVIDE

DISCIPLINE:
MOUNTAIN BIKING

LOCATION:
BANFF, CANADA TO ANTELOPE WELLS, USA

TOUGHNESS FACTOR:
✗✗✗✗✗✗✗✗✗✗

POTENTIAL HAZARDS:
BEARS, MOUNTAIN LIONS, REDNECKS IN PICKUPS

WWW.TOURDIVIDE.ORG

Next time you're out on a bike ride and feeling a little bit weary, spare a thought for the handful of intrepid explorers who have raced their mountain bikes along the Tour Divide—an off-road route along the spine of the Rocky Mountains from Canada to the Mexican border, some 2,745 miles (4,418 km) in all, with high altitude, snow, wildfires, crazy drivers, mountain lions, and grizzly bears to negotiate along the way.

The race takes place every year, normally in mid-June. There's no entry fee, no formal registration, and certainly no prize for winning. It follows a route known as the Great Divide Mountain Bike Route—apparently the world's longest unpaved cycling track—featuring mainly dirt roads and trails from Banff, in Canada, to Antelope Wells, on the US-Mexico border. Riders can tackle it south-to-north or north-to-south, as they please. By the time they finish, they'll have climbed a total of 200,000 vertical feet (61,000 m), and will have crossed the watershed between the Atlantic and Pacific Oceans 28 times.

Mechanics, equipment, and supplies are crucial in a race this long. At times riders are so isolated that they may be as far as 100 miles (160 km) from the nearest store.

"Taking on such an event means a lot more than simply riding your bike a long way," rider Paul Howard tells **Outdoor Fitness** magazine. "The possibility of serious mechanical failure while so far from help requires a decent tool kit and a modicum of mechanical knowhow. A first-aid kit is a pre-requisite, as is being prepared to sleep rough after a 16-hour day in the saddle—not to mention being able to do the same again the next day, and the next..."

Howard planned well and packed prudently before embarking on his race. The essential equipment included sleeping bag, tent, waterproofs, leg- and arm-warmers, hat, gloves, shorts, jerseys, base layers, jacket, socks, shoes, helmet, glasses, camera, two spare inner tubes, a pump, patches, spokes, allen bolts, gaffer tape, a multi-tool, a tire boot, zip ties, four bottle cages and accompanying bottles, and two bike computers. He managed to stash all this in a backpack, a handlebar bag, and on rear panniers. Amazingly, all this was enough to keep him going for the whole length of the Tour Divide.

ABOVE: At times riders are so isolated they may be 100 miles (160 km) from the nearest store

ULTRAMAN WORLD CHAMPIONSHIPS

DISCIPLINE:
SWIMMING, ROAD BIKING, ROAD RUNNING

LOCATION:
HAWAII, USA

TOUGHNESS FACTOR:
✘✘✘✘✘✘✘✘✘✘

POTENTIAL HAZARDS:
JELLYFISH, SEA URCHINS, SHARP CORAL, DEHYDRATION

WWW.ULTRAMANLIVE.COM

"An athletic odyssey of personal rediscovery" is how the Ultraman World Championships—one of the world's most testing triathlons—is sold. And you'd better believe it. This legendary Hawaii sports event is so long it can break the very fittest triathletes. There is a total of 320 miles (515 km) to cover: first the 6.2-mile (10-km) open ocean swim in the sea off Hawaii's Big island; then a 261-mile (420-km) bike ride on the island's roads; finally a 52-mile (84-km) road run.

The event is staged over three days (the bike section is split between day one and day two) but with cut-off times imposed on each stage to eliminate any stragglers. This means there is little time for the athletes to rest up.

Each section offers its own interesting challenges. The swim is especially testing, with triathletes facing brushes with jellyfish or Portuguese man o' war—"whose stings may cause severe discomfort," warn the organizers rather coolly. For that reason, wetsuits are recommended. Ocean swells can be strong, throwing the swimmers about like corks in bottles. And there is the risk of lacerations from sharp outcrops of lava and coral, or spiky sea urchins. "Since stepping on one of these may cause painful and bothersome injury that may even prevent further participation, caution should be exercised when in shallow water," the organizers advise about the latter.

There are plenty of other tests in store, in both the bike and the run sections, as the following competitors recount.

"I felt very sick and nauseous," said Jack Nosco of his bike ordeal. "I threw up several times and was forced to get off and walk— a first for me ever to have had to walk my bike. My wife did a wonderful job in convincing me to continue."

A 2000 competitor, John Girmsey, rested for two hours after exiting the swim but still got into trouble at the start of the bike ride. "The initial long climb took its toll and my legs were cramping," he said. "I started sucking down a lot of salt packets after that to stop the cramps but it took several hours before I had them under control again." On the run section he placed bags of ice under his hat to keep cool. "It proved to be a lifesaver."

Despite Hawaii's clement climate, 1998 competitor Rick Kent found the weather extremely unforgiving on his bike ride. "We encountered some of the most brutal side winds I had ever experienced," he said of his day-one bike section. "You could easily get blown off your bike going down some of the faster descents." The day-two bike ride threw heavy rain, as well as wind, into the

mix. "It was hairy as hell coming down," Kent recalled. "I'm normally pretty fearless in these situations but sanity ruled it out. The rain and wind, along with the severe drop in temperature, made it hard even to ride. I was shaking really badly. All I had on was a sleeveless jersey and shorts. I couldn't even change my hand position to brake."

After winning the 1995 Ultraman, Kevin Cutjar described his ordeal as "much more than a long-distance race. It's a journey! I feel honored to have been among the few who have experienced what has been called one of the most demanding physical challenges ever devised by man."

THE DAY-TWO BIKE RIDE THREW HEAVY RAIN, AS WELL AS WIND, INTO THE MIX. "IT WAS HAIRY AS HELL COMING DOWN"

SELF-TRANSCENDENCE 3,100 MILE RACE

This is officially the longest running race on the planet—by a few thousand country miles. The Self-Transcendence 3,100 Mile Race, staged every summer for 5,649 laps around a city block in New York City, is also surely the world's most boring race.

DISCIPLINE:
ROAD RUNNING

LOCATION:
QUEENS, NEW YORK, USA

TOUGHNESS FACTOR:
✗✗✗✗✗✗✗✗✗✗

POTENTIAL HAZARDS:
DEHYDRATION, HEATSTROKE, MUGGING

WWW.3100.SRICHINMOYRACES.ORG

THE PURPOSE OF THE RACE IS A SPIRITUAL ONE

That's right—5,649 mind-numbing laps around the same city block. Each lap is just over half a mile (883 meters) long, and loops around the perimeter of a high school in the borough of Queens, taking in the stunning views of a children's playground and the Grand Central Parkway. Competitors have 52 days to complete the course, averaging just under 60 miles (96 km) every day, most of them running from 6a.m. until midnight. It's not unusual for competitors to wear out 25 pairs of running shoes by the time the ordeal comes to an end.

"The serious athlete must have tremendous courage, physical stamina, concentration, and the capacity to endure fatigue, boredom, and minor injuries," says the organizer, with more than a little understatement.

There are other more mundane irritants to deal with, such as the Big Apple's summer heat and humidity, its ubiquitous litter and dog poop, its car-exhaust fumes, its vicious mosquitoes, and of course its notoriously rude citizens. At the best of times New Yorkers might struggle to comprehend why anyone would choose to run 3,100 miles around a city block.

In actual fact, the purpose of the race is a spiritual one, with most of the runners being disciples of the late Indian spiritual leader (and athletics advocate and long-distance runner) Sri Chinmoy.

"The cornerstone of Sri Chinmoy's philosophy is the expression of self-transcendence—going beyond personal limits and reaching new levels of inner and outer perfection," explain the race organizers. "Whether it is in the athletic world or any endeavor, for someone to transcend his previous achievements is inner progress and an expression of a new determination, which can only bring us closer to our destined goal: real satisfaction."

At the time of writing, there was real satisfaction for the male and female record-holders of the Self-Transcendence 3,100 Mile Race. The men's record of 41 days and eight hours was held by German runner Madhupran Wolfgang Schwerk; the women's record of 49 days and 14 hours by American Suprabha Beckjord, who enjoys the race so much she has run it over 20 times.

TOUGH MUDDER

Beware of the electric shocks! The most daunting and testing aspect of this global series of obstacle races is something known as Electroshock Therapy.

All 50 or so of the Tough Mudder races staged worldwide include it. Competitors have to run the gauntlet through a gallery of dangling and heavily electrified wires. Whichever route you choose you're going to get zapped by several thousand volts. There's no avoiding it.

"I always run through as fast as possible," says Ben Kirkup, a British man whose CV of Tough Mudder races is well into double figures. "On the head or between the shoulder blades are the worst places you can get zapped. I've taken one on the temple and that was horrific."

There are plenty of other horrific obstacles in store for competitors. As well as running the 10 to 12 miles (16 to 19 km) of the course (depending on which venue you choose), there are physically and mentally demanding tests every mile or so. You jump through rings of fire, you swing along monkey bars, you get gassed, you slither through muddy tubes, you submerge yourself in icy water, and you scale tall fences. Despite the self-inflicted torture, Tough Mudder races are growing in popularity and new events are popping

up across the globe. Designed by British Special Forces, they have tested more than 1.3 million competitors since the launch in 2010. Given all the jumping and the water hazards, injuries are common. At an American Tough Mudder event in 2013, tragically, one man even lost his life.

Teamwork is much more important in this race than individual glory, with all entrants encouraged to help their fellow Tough Mudders negotiate the course. As the organizers state: "The idea of Tough Mudder is not to win...but to have a story to tell."

DISCIPLINE:
OBSTACLE COURSE RACING

LOCATION:
ORIGINALLY PENNSYLVANIA, USA, NOW WORLDWIDE

TOUGHNESS FACTOR:
✖ ✖ ✖ ✖ ✖ ✖ ✖ ✖ ✖ ✖

POTENTIAL HAZARDS:
ELECTROCUTION, BURNS, FREEZING WATER

WWW.TOUGHMUDDER.COM
WWW.SPARTAN.COM
WWW.TOUGHGUY.CO.UK
WWW.WARRIORDASH.COM

There are many other obstacle-course races, similar to Tough Mudder, staged worldwide, with a variety of gruesome ordeals on offer. Tough Guy, Spartan Race, and Warrior Dash are among them.

ABOVE: An entrant is helped by fellow runners through one of the obstacles designed by members of the British Special Forces

DISCIPLINE:
MOUNTAIN RUNNING

LOCATION:
LEADVILLE, COLORADO, USA

TOUGHNESS FACTOR:
✖ ✖ ✖ ✖ ✖ ✖ ✖ ✖ ✖

POTENTIAL HAZARDS:
**DEHYDRATION,
ALTITUDE SICKNESS**

WWW.LEADVILLERACESERIES.COM

Fifty miles (80 km) out, 50 miles back. It sounds so simple on paper. But when you're out on those Rocky Mountain trails, in the dust, the sweat, the rain, the heat, and the thin air–climbing from 9,200 ft (2,800 m) to the 12,600 ft (3,840 m) Hope Pass and back again–nothing seems simple. American runner Tina Lewis won the 2012 Leadville Trail 100 in 19 hours and 33 minutes.

Her achievement involved an awful lot of suffering since she finds that running at altitude often causes her stomach to malfunction. "Something with the altitude," she explained to ultramarathon website iRunFar.com. "My stomach just locks down and then I can't eat and I end up throwing up."

The Leadville Trail 100 was first set up by former miner Kenneth Chlouber in an effort to inject a bit of life into the ailing mining town of Leadville. "You're crazy! You'll kill someone!" warned staff at the local hospital when Chlouber told them about his project. He responded: "Well, then we will be famous, won't we?" No one has actually died on the Leadville Trail 100 (yet!) but Chlouber achieved the fame he desired all the same. The race is now considered a classic among America's, and indeed the world's, top ultramarathoners.

At the time of writing, the course record is held by Matt Carpenter, who finished the 2005 race in 15 hours and 42 minutes. In his younger days Carpenter had his VO^2 Max (the body's ability to deliver oxygen to the muscles) recorded at 90.2, and his standing heart rate at 33 beats a minute—staggeringly fit by anyone's standards. His nickname is "The Lung." And his attitude to training? "I've been known to wake up in the middle of the night and go back out if I think I could give it just a little more," he says. That's the kind of attitude you need to be a winner at Leadville.

ABOVE: The Colorado Rockies provide a stunning yet testing backdrop for this epic race

RACE ACROSS AMERICA

DISCIPLINE:
ROAD CYCLING

LOCATION:
**OCEANSIDE, CALIFORNIA TO
ANNAPOLIS, MARYLAND, USA**

TOUGHNESS FACTOR:
✖✖✖✖✖✖✖✖✖✖

POTENTIAL HAZARDS:
**CAR CRASH,
SLEEP DEPRIVATION,
DEHYDRATION**

WWW.RACEACROSSAMERICA.ORG

It's 30 percent longer than the Tour de France. Although the course of the infamous Race Across America varies slightly from year to year, one feature that stubbornly remains the same is the fact that competitors need to cycle around 3,000 miles (4,800 km) across the entire continent of North America, always west to east. The Tour de France is around 2,300 miles (3,700 km) by comparison. And unlike the professional French race, which is split into stages, the RAAM has no official stops: competitors often ride through the night, averaging only an hour and a half of sleep every day.

The top riders complete their transcontinental marathon across 12 states (including 170,000 ft/ 51,820 m of climbing) in under nine days, so imagine the exhaustion and sleep deprivation they must suffer from. Motor traffic is a constant risk, too. Several riders have been killed or injured while competing.

In 2014, Austrian cyclist Christoph Strasser broke the race record, crossing America in a Lycra-grinding seven days, 15 hours, and 56 minutes. He said the toughest aspect of the race was the constant lack of sleep. Some nights he had less than half an hour of shut-eye. "Tiredness is part of the game," he told cycling website Velocrushindia.com. "You need a good crew to keep you in a good mood, make jokes, talk a lot, give you good company, and never leave you alone with your thoughts."

Another test for RAAM cyclists is the variation in climate throughout the race. In the desert regions, temperatures can reach 104°F (40°C), calling for up to 1.5 gallons (6 liters) of drinking water every hour. In the high Rocky Mountains, on the other hand, cyclists need to don winter clothes. "You enjoy the cold temperatures, because it will get hot again in the next days," Strasser says. Backed up by a highly efficient support team, Strasser planned any bike changes (switching from road bike to time-trial bike, for example, to take advantage of the road conditions) with military precision. And if a mechanical adjustment was necessary, he would always use the pit stop to attend to other housekeeping matters. "We stop and everything gets done at the same time: new Garmin device, new drink bottles, toilet, ass cream, sun cream," he explains. "While I go for a pee, one of the crew puts sun cream on my head, another one changes the wheel and puts oil on the chain, and another one changes the battery of the lights and the [communication] device. The whole stop takes 45 seconds."

Even when there are 3,000 miles to cycle, record-breakers still need to make their pit stops as brief as possible.

BELOW: Runners are expected to be self-sufficient and must carry pack equipment not just for running, but also for camping

BELOW: Runners are expected to be self-sufficient and must carry pack equipment not just for running, but also for camping

Photo courtesy of Grand to Grand Ultra

GRAND TO GRAND ULTRA

DISCIPLINE:
RUNNING

LOCATION:
NORTH RIM, ARIZONA TO GRAND STAIRCASE, UTAH, USA

TOUGHNESS FACTOR:
✗✗✗✗✗✗✗ ✗✗✗

POTENTIAL HAZARDS:
SNAKES, SCORPIONS, DEHYDRATION

WWW.G2GULTRA.COM

From the edge of the Grand Canyon in Arizona, along the rock layers of the Grand Staircase, 170 miles (274 km) to the cliffs of southern Utah—it's called the Grand to Grand Ultra. Six stages run over seven days, camping in tents each night. You don't get grander than this. The course of this ultramarathon twists and turns across desert, over sand dunes, along forest trails, up rocky escarpments, past mesas, buttes, and hoodoo rock formations, and through steep-sided canyons.

The race is self-supported so all runners must carry their own equipment and supplies. The list of mandatory items includes backpack, sleeping bag, sleeping mat, jacket, compass, knife, signal mirror, whistle, space blanket, headlamps, flashing lights, water containers, blister kit, and a minimum of 2,000 calories of food for each day of the race.

British runner Lee Stobbs competed in the 2014 event. Halfway through the race, the lack of sleep began to take its toll: "Exasperated and dangerously dehydrated, I began to experience mild hallucinations— mistaking a distant tree for a car, for example—which was a sign that I needed to refuel and rest," he wrote in **GQ** magazine. He was also suffering from a knee injury. He came very close to throwing in the towel until he was inspired by the words of a fellow competitor—"Our bodies will always give up," he said, "but the body is never tired if the mind is not tired."

Stobbs soldiered on, eventually reaching the race finish after a grueling 70 hours and nine minutes. "The sight of the finishing tape, with the pink cliffs decorating the horizon, will remain etched in my memory forever. Weary, wounded, and physically defunct, my lifeless legs dropped at the line as I looked up to see my finisher's medal there in waiting. I may have been broken but I never felt more alive."

ABOVE: Slot canyons are just one of the many geographical features competitors have to tackle

6633 ULTRA

DISCIPLINE:
RUNNING AND HIKING

LOCATION:
EAGLE PLAINS, YUKON TO TUKTOYAKTUK, NORTHERN TERRITORIES, CANADA

TOUGHNESS FACTOR:
✗✗✗✗✗✗✗✗ ✗ ✗

POTENTIAL HAZARDS:
EXPOSURE, FREEZING TO DEATH

WWW.6633ULTRA.COM

If you like it cold, and you like it windy, you'll love the 6633 Ultra. This foot race takes competitors from Eagle Plains, in the Canadian territory of Yukon, 350 miles (563 km) all the way to Tuktoyaktuk, in the Northwest Territories, on the shores of the Arctic Ocean. It crosses some of the bleakest, most pristine (and coldest and windiest) terrain in the Great White North. "This race is only for big boys and girls," the organizers warn.

Competitors either carry or pull on sleds all the provisions they need during the race, including food, cooking equipment, spare clothing, and sleeping gear. They are allowed to camp and prepare food at checkpoints along the way. Just 23 miles (37 km) after the start of the race, they cross into Canada's Arctic Circle, and it's not long before they become very exposed to the elements. One long stretch of the route is nicknamed Hurricane Alley, with vicious winds—known as katabatic winds—coming down off the Arctic ice sheets. "When the winds are blowing, the road is usually closed to vehicles," the organizers explain. "Lorries using the [highway] are regularly blown over. Any human caught in these winds could quite literally be forced to crawl."

Given such conditions, no wonder the list of recommended equipment is exhaustive. Aside from all the cold-weather gear you'd expect to wear in the Arctic Circle, race organizers suggest the following essential items: hydration pack with insulated hose, balaclava, Neoprene face mask, head torch, goggles, flashing beacon, lip cream, knife, hand warmers, extra-thick sleeping bag, foam mat, cooker, fuel, kettle, wind shelter, blister plasters, rope, plus lots of dehydrated food. You've been warned!

The course record for the 6633 Ultra is held by a very accomplished ultrarunner called Mimi Anderson who, in 2007, completed the route in 143 hours and 25 minutes. "This race was a real challenge," she wrote in her race blog on marvellousmimi.com. "What a shock it was—temperatures averaging -40°F (-40°C) and, on one of the days, going as low as -100°F (-75°C) with the wind chill factor." About 200 miles (320 km) into the race, suffering from a serious lack of sleep and with 150 torturous miles still to go, Anderson started to hallucinate. "I saw an elephant, hundreds of men on skidoos about to attack me, men carrying guns standing near parked cars," she wrote. "I even closed my eyes and counted to ten knowing that none of this was real. On opening my eyes they were still there and had moved. It was like being in a movie."

The bitter cold also took its toll on Anderson. "The one part of my body I found very difficult to keep warm were my hands," she wrote. "In order to eat or get something out of my sled, I had to take my over-mitts off. In a matter of 30 seconds my fingertips felt like blocks of ice. They would take 15 minutes to defrost."

If 350 miles (563 km) of this sounds unbearable then there's always a shorter race on offer— a mere 120 miles (193 km). Equally windy and equally cold, of course.

ABOVE: A glimpse of aurora borealis, or Northern Lights, makes a change from the frozen white landscape that competitors usually see

DISCIPLINE:
MOUNTAIN RUNNING

LOCATION:
SQUAW VALLEY TO AUBURN, CALIFORNIA, USA

TOUGHNESS FACTOR:
✕✕✕✕✕✕✕ ✕ ✕ ✕

POTENTIAL HAZARDS:
BROKEN LIMBS, HEAT EXHAUSTION, DEHYDRATION, SNAKEBITE

WWW.WSER.ORG

They've been running the Western States since 1974. Following the central section of the Western States Trail, an ancient Native American route through the Rockies, this 100-mile (160-km) ultramarathon has achieved legendary status—mainly because it's run non-stop through the night, but also because it covers some of the wildest, toughest, and roughest mountain trails in the United States. It's a similar route to the Tevis Cup equestrian race (see page 26).

ABOVE: Runners are advised to carry a water-filtration pump in case their water runs out

...YOU COULD BE WAITING IN PAIN FOR A VERY LONG TIME BEFORE GETTING EVACUATED

The race starts close to the California/Nevada state line in the town of Squaw Valley—normally at 5a.m. in the last weekend of June. Runners have until 11a.m. the following day to reach the finish line in Auburn, California, after running over high mountain passes, and through deep, dark canyons.

"Remember that much of this territory is accessible only by foot, horse or helicopter," warn the organizers. In other words, if you break a bone (which has been known to happen), you could be waiting in pain for a very long time before getting evacuated by the emergency services. Before starting the race, all runners are advised to stock up with ample fluids and food supplies, and a water filtration pump in case their water supplies run out. "The remoteness of the trail can lead to disaster for anyone not experienced in the backwoods," they are warned. Flashlights are essential since much of the trail is run in the pitch dark of night. "If your lights fail, wait for another runner with a light," competitors are warned. "Do not try to find your way in the dark. If you are the last runner, wait for the search-and-rescue sweep teams." Runners spend much of their time either straining uphill or careering downhill. Altogether there are 18,000 ft

(5,486 m) of climbing and 23,000 ft (7,010 m) of descending, plus a chilly rope crossing of the American River. Then there's the weather to contend with. Even though this is midsummer, it's high in the Rocky Mountains. The temperature can be as bone chilling as 20°F (-6°C), or as sweltering as 110°F (43°C).

Back in 1985 the **Los Angeles Times** published a eulogy to the Western States and later read it out at the annual flag-raising ceremony for the race: "Along the Emigrant Trail of granite clefts, majestic forests, and pristine streams, we will feel the presence of the Paiute Indians, the mountain men, gold miners, and pioneer families," they proclaimed. "As morning gives way to afternoon in the lower elevations, where oaks and grasses replace the tall pines of the ridges and where

rivulets merge into the defined forks of the American River, we will encounter the oppressive Central Valley heat working its way up the canyons. When dark and coolness come, our way along the silent trail will be marked only by flashlight and the distant lights of Auburn."

At the time of writing, the record for the Western States is held by Timothy Olson who, in 2012, completed the course in 14 hours and 46 minutes. Olson famously came to long-distance running after a long period of drug addiction. He says running gave him the strength to abandon the drugs. "I breathe fresh air. I look at the grass, trees, and, sometimes, snow," he told Meghan Hicks in **Competitor** magazine. "I am in the present moment. I feel peace. I am free."

ABOVE: Competitors must complete the course in 30 hours or less. Those finishing in under 24 hours receive a silver belt buckle as a prize

APPALACHIAN TRAIL

The Appalachian Trail is essentially a footpath. But no ordinary footpath. As author Bill Bryson writes in **A Walk in the Woods**, his biographical account of attempting to hike the entire 2,180-mile (3,500-km) route through the eastern United States, "the Appalachian Trail is the granddaddy of long hikes." "From Georgia to Maine," he continues, "it wanders across fourteen states, through plump, comely hills whose very names—Blue Ridge, Smokies, Cumberlands, Catskills, Green Mountains, White Mountains—seem an invitation to amble."

DISCIPLINE:
HIKING

LOCATION:
SPRINGER MOUNTAIN, GEORGIA TO MOUNT KATAHDIN, MAINE, USA

TOUGHNESS FACTOR:
✖ ✖ ✖ ✖ ✖ ✖ ✖ ✖ ✖

POTENTIAL HAZARDS:
BEARS, SNAKES, HEAT EXHAUSTION, EXPOSURE

WWW.APPALACHIANTRAIL.ORG

What Bryson didn't bank on (along with the vast majority of Appalachian Trail hikers) was the gargantuan scale of the trail. In fact he failed to hike it all, skipping sections, abandoning for periods of time, returning for various legs, and again abandoning.

The most intrepid hikers attempt to walk the entire Appalachian Trail in a single season. They are known as "thru-hikers," as opposed to "section-hikers" who split their hike into separate legs. Typically they will walk south to north, starting in Georgia in spring and finishing in Maine in fall. Apparently only around a quarter of those who start actually reach the end. Most, like Bryson, are unable to stay the distance. Nonetheless, the Appalachian Trail Conservancy estimates that well over 15,000 determined walkers have completed the entire trail since it was inaugurated in the 1930s.

The route is not without its hazards. Black bears, rattlesnakes, copperheads, water moccasins, wild boars, rutting moose, and unfriendly dogs roam the trail. But most lethal of all are other human beings. Over the years a handful of hikers have been murdered while attempting the trail. The Appalachian Trail Conservancy advises against hiking alone. There are more than 250 shelters and campsites along the route—most very basic, some more substantial, and a few offering proper lodging and catering in the summer months. Many hikers stock up on provisions at the towns through which the trail passes.

At the time of writing, the record time for completing the entire trail in one go is held by American hiker Jennifer Pharr Davis. In 2011, helped by a support team, she speed-hiked over 2,000 miles (3,300 km) in a thigh-busting 46 days and 11 hours—that's an average of around 47 miles (76 km) a day. Most days she would start hiking at sunrise, usually around 5a.m., pushing on throughout the entire day until 10p.m., making use of all possible daylight. During her record attempt, asked what kept her going, she said it was the wild animals that she spotted along the trail. Moose, bears, porcupine, skunks, and "lots of little critters" kept her company. "Any time I've seen a moose or a bear, it's like taking a little energy pill," she told the **New York Times**.

RIGHT: A hiker struggles up Mount Katahdin in Maine. Only a quarter of those who start the trail reach the end

AUSABLE RIVER CANOE MARATHON

There's quite a history to this annual race. It was all the way back in 1947 that the first AuSable River Canoe Marathon took place. Since then the event has firmly cemented its place in paddle-sport folklore.

It's a non-stop race, featuring teams of two, that starts at night in the town of Grayling, Michigan, and finishes 120 miles (193 km) later near the shores of Lake Huron, in Oscoda, Michigan. But it's the start of the race that is perhaps most surprising of all: competitors have to run with their canoes several blocks through the city streets of Grayling before they put in at the river.

What follows is a night- and daytime odyssey along the Au Sable River, twisting through the forests of Michigan, including some very tricky portage sections. "Contestants must navigate the narrow, winding upper stretch in total darkness, as well as stump-filled ponds and the blazing July sun in the lower stretch," explain the organizers. "They must be in peak condition in order to complete the race in the allotted time, and to endure the grueling and strenuous physical and mental strains." At the time of writing, the race record of 13 hours and 58 minutes is held by Canadian canoeists Serge Corbin and Solomon Carriere. In 2005, Corbin (this time teamed with Jeff Kolka) was involved in the most dramatic

finish the event has ever seen. Unbelievably, after nearly 15 hours and 50,000 paddle strokes, they found themselves sprinting toward the finish line neck-and-neck with a rival all-American team. They won by a single second.

Jeff Kolka paid tribute to his teammate Corbin when the latter was inducted into the race's hall of fame. "Serge Corbin is probably the greatest paddler that ever lived," he said. "He's very serious and passionate about what he does, and he's managed to do stuff nobody else has ever done. And I don't think anybody will for a very long time."

Kolka said it wasn't just Corbin's physical power that put him ahead of his rivals. "You can measure a lot of physical capabilities in a person—VO^2 max and their strength—but sometimes it comes down to heart. That's what will pull you through more than anything else: the mental will and heart you put into something."

DISCIPLINE:
CANOEING

LOCATION:
AU SABLE RIVER, MICHIGAN, USA

TOUGHNESS FACTOR:
✖ ✖ ✖ ✖ ✖ ✖ ✖ ✖ ✖

POTENTIAL HAZARDS:
CAPSIZING, DROWNING

WWW.AUSABLECANOEMARATHON.ORG

BELOW: It might look peaceful out on the water, but the effort needed to complete all 120 miles (193 km) pushes even the most experienced canoeists to the limits of their abilities

A trek of 1,000 miles (1,609 km) across the snowy wastes of the very north of North America, the Yukon Quest is a gruesomely tough sled-dog race held during the coldest weeks of winter. It's tough on the mushers, and it's tough on the dogs. It's tough just reading about it.

DISCIPLINE:
SLED-DOG RACING

LOCATION:
WHITEHORSE, YUKON, CANADA TO FAIRBANKS, ALASKA, USA

TOUGHNESS FACTOR:
✖✖✖✖✖✖✖✖✖

POTENTIAL HAZARDS:
HYPOTHERMIA, FROSTBITE, SNOWSTORMS

WWW.YUKONQUEST.COM

The race route runs between Fairbanks, in the US state of Alaska, and Whitehorse, in the Canadian territory of Yukon (swapping direction every year in order to keep things interesting). It follows the course of an old gold prospectors' supply route called the Klondike Highway. Wind speeds can reach 50 mph (80 km/h), and temperatures can drop so low that even the fuel in the local snowmobiles freezes.

The real stars of the race are the Alaskan huskies powering the sleds. "They have been bred for generations for their endurance, strength, speed, tough feet, good attitude and appetites, and most importantly their desire to pull in harness, and their abilities to run well within a team," the race organizers explain.

The first Yukon Quest took place in February 1984 when 26 teams paid $500 to start the event, and 20 eventually reached the finish line. The winner that year was Sonny Lindner, posting a time of just over 12 days.

Fast-forward to the modern day and race champion is Brent Sass. In 2015 he won in just nine days and 12 hours. At one point in the race, Sass was enjoying a 10-hour lead over his nearest rival, Allen Moore. But, stopping to rest, he accidentally overslept and discovered Moore had overtaken him. Nevertheless, he later managed to catch up and win the race. "It works!" he said after his triumph. "Fall asleep on the trail for ten hours and you can come in first."

There have been various mishaps over the years. In 2006 six mushers and their teams had to be rescued by helicopter. In 2011 an experienced musher nearly died after falling through ice into a freezing-cold pond.

Moore, who won in 2014, summed up the Quest's attraction: "It's for the adventure," he said. "While we're doing it we sometimes wonder why. But as soon as we get off of it, we forget and can't wait to do it again."

ABOVE: Alaskan huskies are bred for their endurance, strength, speed, tough feet, attitude, appetite, and teamwork.

CHAPTER 2

EUROPE

THE GR 20

Corsica is one of the Mediterranean's wildest islands, and stretching for 110 miles (180 km) north-to-south along its middle, like a dragon's backbone, is an impressive string of mountain ridges, regularly rising well over 6,500 ft (2,000 m). On top of this ridge runs a rocky path known as the GR 20 (GR stands for Grande Randonnée, or Great Hike), arguably the most challenging long-distance path in Europe.

DISCIPLINE:
HIKING, SCRAMBLING

LOCATION:
ACROSS CORSICA

TOUGHNESS FACTOR:
✖ ✖ ✖ ✖ ✖ ✖ ✖ ✖ ✖

POTENTIAL HAZARDS:
FALLING ROCKS

WWW.VISIT-CORSICA.COM

It's a real classic, a prominent feature on any serious hiker's bucket list. Many intrepid hill walkers and mountain runners have attempted it, but by no means all have succeeded. It's quite an undertaking—one that requires physical fitness, mental fortitude, and up to 15 days of steep hiking and scrambling over rocks. Nights are spent either in the very basic mountain huts along the route, or wild camping. The total elevation along the route is almost 40,000 ft (more than 12,000 m). "The GR 20 is merciless," says one serious hiker who knows the trail very well. "You need to be prepared to rough it up. Period."

Rough it up indeed. Sometimes the French Foreign Legion—no strangers to roughing it—use the GR 20 as a long-distance training route. Apparently they are expected to complete it in around seven days, lugging all their equipment on their backs, of course.

Professional mountain runners can't resist the wild rugged terrain of the Corsican mountains either. The current world record for the GR 20 was set in the summer of 2014 by 28-year-old local Guillaume Peretti. What takes us mere mortals 15 days, he completed in a staggering 32 hours. "It's really, really difficult," he panted just minutes after reaching the end. "You must realize that I really suffered during the final hours. Constant suffering, pain everywhere, especially in my knees. But you have to keep going, regardless."

BELOW: The circuit follows this rugged hiking path that winds its way around the mountain

ULTRA-TRAIL DU MONT-BLANC

More than two thousand runners line up to start this Alpine ultramarathon every year. Their race route runs 103 miles (166 km), close to a famous old hiking path known as the Tour du Mont Blanc, looping wide around Europe's tallest mountain. Although the exact course changes slightly every year, it normally starts and finishes in the French ski resort of Chamonix, crossing the frontier into both Italy and Switzerland on the way.

DISCIPLINE:
MOUNTAIN RUNNING

LOCATION:
FRANCE, ITALY, AND SWITZERLAND

TOUGHNESS FACTOR:
✗✗✗✗✗✗ ✗ ✗ ✗

POTENTIAL HAZARDS:
INTENSE HEAT, INTENSE COLD

WWW.ULTRATRAILMB.COM

The total elevation gain is normally close to 32,800 ft (10,000 m). The race is famous for the solidarity displayed among competitors. All runners are expected to "make it their priority to help any other person in danger or in difficulty." And with hazards described by the organizers as ranging from "snow, hail, fog, heat (more than 86°F/30°C) or intense cold (less than 14°F/-10°C), with or without a violent wind," danger and difficulty are never far away.

Legendary Catalan mountain runner Kilian Jornet has won the event a total of three times. In 2011 he posted an amazing time of 20 hours and 36 minutes. Brought up in a mountain village in the Pyrenees, Jornet has a deep respect for the mountains he runs on. "We must understand mountains are much stronger than us," he says. "Compared to the age of the mountain, we are nothing. We are really small." He says that when he's racing up and down the steep slopes, he feels the mountain is like his "dancing partner." Watch him in fast descent mode and you'll see him adjust his arms and hands like a squirrel moves its tail while leaping from branch to branch. "When you're running downhill, it's not just about moving your legs," he explains. "You must use your upper body, arms, and hands, too. Your body goes side-to-side, leans back, leans forward. You move your arms to find the balance and change your center of gravity."

But most surprising of all is Jornet's downhill training method. One of his techniques is to memorize the terrain in front of him, close his eyes, and continue running blind for distances of up to 150 ft (50 m). "What's important is the connection between your vision and the movement of your muscles," he says. "You don't look exactly where you are placing your feet. You look at the trail ahead of you and memorize the trail so that you place your feet in the right place." That takes an awful lot of practice. And when you're running up and down the trails of Mont Blanc, it's not always wise to keep your eyes shut.

ALL RUNNERS ARE EXPECTED TO "MAKE IT THEIR PRIORITY TO HELP ANY OTHER PERSON IN DANGER OR IN DIFFICULTY"

THE ENGLISH CHANNEL SWIM

DISCIPLINE:
OCEAN SWIMMING

LOCATION:
THE ENGLISH CHANNEL, BETWEEN ENGLAND AND FRANCE

TOUGHNESS FACTOR:
✗✗✗✗✗✗✗✗ ✗ ✗

POTENTIAL HAZARDS:
HYPOTHERMIA, JELLYFISH STINGS, DROWNING

WWW.CHANNELSWIMMINGASSOCIATION.COM

The English Channel may be just 21 miles (34 km) wide at its narrowest point (on a clear day you can see all the way across), yet it has proved far too mighty a challenge for many an unwary swimmer. The lion's share of swim-powered crossings are attempted northwest to southeast, from Shakespeare's Cliff or Samphire Hoe (in between Folkestone and Dover on the English side) to Cap Gris Nez (in between Boulogne and Calais on the French side)—a stretch of water known as the Strait of Dover.

"IT IS A LIVING THING. YOU NEVER KNOW WHAT SORT OF CONDITIONS YOU ARE GOING TO MEET OUT THERE."

As well as the 21 miles (34 km) of sea to plow through, there are added hazards. First off, swimmers must take into account the very strong currents, often pushing them well over the official distance by the time they reach the French shore. The water can be cold, even in summer, with waves sometimes reaching more than 6 ft (2 m) high. The Channel Swimming Association (the official body that governs this rather eccentric sporting feat) also warns that "jellyfish, seaweed, and the occasional plank of wood" can put you off your stroke.

If you want your effort to be recorded as an official crossing, then wetsuits aren't permitted. Instead, swimmers smear their bodies with grease. And grease offers little protection from either stinging tentacles or planks of wood. Bear in mind, too, that the English Channel is one of the busiest shipping channels in the world, with more than 600 tankers and 200 ferries negotiating its waters every single day. For safety reasons, all swimmers need to be accompanied by a pilot boat. It's that or risk being swamped by a passing 500,000-tonne supertanker.

The first recorded cross-channel swim was all the way back in 1875 by a certain Captain Matthew Webb. On August 25, on his second attempt, he swam from Admiralty Pier, in Dover, to Calais in 21 hours and 45 minutes. Despite being helped by three support boats and a generous all-over smearing of porpoise oil, Webb was forced by sea currents to zigzag his way across the channel. He swam 40 miles (64 km) in all, and picked up a fair few jellyfish stings for his troubles, but ended up one of the most famous sports celebrities of his era. A Victorian Michael Phelps, you might say. After his sporting feat he was in constant demand for swimming exhibitions and galas. And all sorts of Captain Matthew Webb official memorabilia—books, pottery, matches, dinner sets—were made available for his adoring fans.

Webb's last ever stunt, and arguably his most audacious, was an attempt in 1883 to traverse the treacherous rapids of the Niagara River below Niagara Falls. Shortly after embarking on his swim he was pulled under. His drowned corpse was found four days later downstream. A memorial in his home village of Dawley, in the English county of Shropshire, simply says: "Nothing great is easy."

Ever since those initial Victorian toes in the water, hundreds of different swimmers have successfully crossed the English Channel. At the time of writing (according to the Channel Swimming Association) there have been more than 1,900 solo crossings made by over 1,400 people. The record time is held by Australia's Trent Grimsey (six hours, 55 minutes), while the record number—a staggering 43 crossings—is held by Dover resident Alison Streeter, aka Queen of the Channel. "It has a unique fascination," she says of the watery gap between England and France. "It is a living thing. You never know what sort of conditions you are going to meet out there."

RACE THE TRAIN

There's something reassuringly British and eccentric about Race the Train. Featuring an old-fashioned steam train, a Welsh seaside town called Tywyn, and a cross-country course over the hills and dales of Snowdonia, it's not your everyday running race.

DISCIPLINE:
CROSS-COUNTRY RUNNING

LOCATION:
SNOWDONIA, WALES

TOUGHNESS FACTOR:
✖ ✖ ✖ ✖ ✖ ✖ ✖ ✖ ✖ ✖ ✖

POTENTIAL HAZARDS:
TRAIN COLLISION

WWW.RACETHETRAIN.COM

Steam train and runners all set off at the same time, with the railway track (of the narrow-gauge Talyllyn Railway) and the running course following a similar route northeast into Snowdonia National Park, and back to Tywyn again. As the runners struggle across the mixture of roads, tracks, footpaths, and farmland, the train passengers lean out of their windows yelling encouragement. Steam power may pull them along faster than leg power propels the runners, but the various station stops along the route give the stronger runners a chance to catch up, even overtake. Competitors must keep their pace up at all times—one eye on the boggy trail, and the other on their nemesis, puffing and whistling alongside them. The train normally takes around an hour and 48 minutes to complete its route from Tywyn to Abergynolwyn, and back again. Accomplished cross-country runners should beat it to the finish line with minutes to spare. Indeed, in 2014, of the 1,400 or so finishers, 188 of them beat the train. The race distance is 14 miles (22.5 km).

In 2013, Londoner Tobias Mews took on this man-versus-machine challenge. Frustrated at his daily commute in the big city, and the number of trains he had barely missed during the course of his working life, he decided to exact his revenge by racing the Talyllyn Railway. "Any notion I have of staying ahead of the train soon disappears," he wrote in **Metro** newspaper of his experience. "Fifteen minutes into the race, I hear the steam train chugging behind me, as if chanting: 'I'm coming to get you, I'm coming to get you...' and mockingly blowing its whistle. With my heart beating like a hunted deer's, and the rain pouring down,

the next 30 minutes play out like a game of cat-and-mouse as I pursue the train, bounding over fields, wading across streams, and trudging through bogs." Tobias persisted, however, and eventually beat the train by an impressive 18 minutes.

Race the Train has been staged every year since 1984, with an increasing number of runners each year attempting to reach the finish line before the engine.

ABOVE: The train making its way up into Snowdonia National Park

TALISKER WHISKY ATLANTIC CHALLENGE

They call it "The World's Toughest Rowing Race." Since competitors have to cross the entire Atlantic Ocean on oar power alone, it's a fair boast. First staged in 1997, the Atlantic Rowing Race (currently known as the Talisker Whisky Atlantic Challenge) sees teams of two or four braving the ocean waves between the Canary Islands and the West Indies for a distance of around 2,930 miles (4,700 km).

DISCIPLINE:
ROWING

LOCATION:
THE CANARY ISLANDS TO THE WEST INDIES

TOUGHNESS FACTOR:
✘✘✘✘✘✘✘✘✘

POTENTIAL HAZARDS:
STORMS, CAPSIZING, SUNBURN, SALT RASH, BODY SORES

WWW.TALISKERWHISKYATLANTICCHALLENGE.COM

The rules insist that all competing boats are designed similarly—self-righting (in case of capsize), with a small cabin, GPS technology, tracking beacons, and a satellite phone. Despite all these mod cons, during their time at sea the rowers must face all sorts of hardships, ranging from enormous waves, storms, and seasickness, to salt rash, sleep deprivation, and body sores in the most likely (and unlikely) places. To avoid unnecessary chafing, many competitors choose to strip off completely while they're rowing. After all, there's no one around to complain.

Britons Tom Salt and Mike Burton won the 2013 Atlantic Challenge in a time of 41 days, two hours and 38 minutes. Arriving in the Caribbean island of Antigua, lean of body, bronzed of skin and hirsute of face, they told how they had rowed their vessel Locura Rows the Atlantic in shifts of two hours on, two hours off, dealing with 40 ft (12 m) waves, a capsize, and an encounter with a 20 ft (6 m) marlin that managed to spear a small hole in their hull.

"We're no strangers to extreme challenges," Tom said afterward, "but this is definitely the hardest thing we've ever done and it pushed us to new limits both physically and mentally."

BELOW: A British crew set off on course for the West Indies, just under 3,000 miles (4,7000 km) away

THE IRISH CHANNEL SWIM

Of all the Ocean's Seven swims (see page 19), the North Channel—between Northern Ireland and Scotland—is considered the toughest. Not only is it long (21.5 miles/35 km), but it's cold (down to 50°F/10°C), windy (up to force six), choppy (waves as high as 6 ft/2 m), busy (there are multiple ferries every day), and riddled with Lion's Mane jellyfish, which can give very nasty stings.

DISCIPLINE:
OCEAN SWIMMING

LOCATION:
THE NORTH CHANNEL, BETWEEN NORTHERN IRELAND AND SCOTLAND

TOUGHNESS FACTOR:
✗✗✗✗✗✗✗ ✗ ✗

POTENTIAL HAZARDS:
HYPOTHERMIA, JELLYFISH, DROWNING

WWW.ILDSA.INFO

"FROM THE MOMENT I STARTED UNTIL THE MOMENT I FINISHED, I WAS STUNG REPEATEDLY"

Unfortunately, if you want your swim to be officially recognized, you cannot wear a wetsuit. "You will get stung," warns the Irish Long-Distance Swimming Association, in no uncertain terms. "You are going to come across blooms of Lion's Mane jellyfish when swimming, and it will soon be clear that there are too many to be able to swim around. Just hope for a sunny day as this will help to drive them deeper into the water, just low enough for you to miss them."

One swimmer, Ed Williams, had to abandon his swim in 2014 after suffering multiple stings on every part of his body, even inside his mouth. "The calm water meant that jellyfish were out in their thousands at the surface of the water," he remembers. "From the moment I started until the moment I finished, I was stung repeatedly. These are not your everyday jellyfish. They are ferocious red beasts and their stings affect the nervous system and inflict huge amounts of pain. I was vomiting repeatedly and my muscles were going into spasm, which are all big warning signs for a severe jellyfish reaction before things turn life threatening. I'm pretty resilient, but I honesty felt on the verge of death, so reluctantly I called it quits."

Alison Streeter has completed the crossing three times. On her first attempt it was jellyfish and cold water that thwarted her. Her mother had to pull her from the water after she fell unconscious. "But for Mum I'd be at the bottom of the North Channel," she recalls. "The jellyfish there are lethal. These buggers swim upside down and come right at you."

54° 44' 12.08" N, 5° 19' 29.27" W

ENDUROMAN ARCH TO ARC

London has its famous Marble Arch. Paris has its even more famous Arc de Triomphe. The two landmarks are 213 miles (343 km) apart as the crow flies, with lots of countryside and, of course, the English Channel in between them. Surely it's not possible to race from one to the other by running, cycling, and swimming? Au contraire. Truly intrepid athletes take part in a race called the Enduroman Arch to Arc triathlon. It must be one of the longest and most daunting point-to-point triathlons on the planet.

DISCIPLINE:
RUNNING, SWIMMING, ROAD CYCLING

LOCATION:
LONDON, ENGLAND TO PARIS, FRANCE

TOUGHNESS FACTOR:
✖✖✖✖✖✖✖✖✖✖

POTENTIAL HAZARDS:
CROSS-CHANNEL FERRIES, HYPOTHERMIA

WWW.ENDUROMAN.COM

The odyssey starts off with an 87-mile (140-km) run from central London's Marble Arch to Dover, on the Kent coast. Then comes the toughest bit—the swim across the English Channel to France (at least 21 miles/34 km, depending on sea currents). Finally, there's the 181-mile (290-km) bike ride to Paris.

At the time of writing, less than 20 athletes have ever completed the challenge. The world record is held by Australian swimming coach John Van Wisse. London to Dover he ran in just under 16 hours. His cross-channel swim took 12 and a half hours and his bike ride to Paris was completed in 14 hours. Factor in the obligatory waits at the transitions and you get an overall time of 61 hours and 27 minutes. Not as fast as Eurostar but impressive all the same, especially since, at one point, Van Wisse got lost in the suburbs of London, adding some unnecessary extra miles to his route. He also had to withstand tempestuous conditions during his cross-channel swim, continuing despite the contrary advice of his pilot boatman, and being mistaken for an illegal immigrant by the UK authorities. "It was a real roller-coaster," he said afterward. "There was a time I contemplated pulling out. I was upset that I had got such a bad hand but then I thought I did all this training and stopped feeling sorry for myself."

Van Wisse told ABC News about his strategy for breaking the record. "I just went as hard as I could the whole way," he said. "It was a roundabout of emotions and events and dramas. It was like a soap series—all different things happening."

ABOVE: On its own, the 181-mile ride (290-km) from Calais to Paris is a test of fitness. Imagine attempting that distance having run 87 miles (140 km) and swum 21 miles (34 km) beforehand

VASALOPPET

In 1520 a young Scandinavian nobleman called Gustav Ericsson Vasa found himself fleeing from the soldiers of King Christian II (aka Christian the Tyrant), the Danish ruler of Scandinavia. Vasa's parents, along with much of the Swedish aristocracy, had been massacred by the king. In fear of his life, young Vasa cross-country skied west across most of Sweden toward the Norwegian border.

DISCIPLINE:
CROSS-COUNTRY SKIING

LOCATION:
SÄLEN TO MORA, SWEDEN

TOUGHNESS FACTOR:
✖✖✖✖✖✖ ✖ ✖ ✖ ✖

POTENTIAL HAZARDS:
HYPOTHERMIA

WWW.VASALOPPET.SE

Eventually, he led an uprising against the occupying Danes, and established Sweden as an independent nation. Vasa's original escape route—between the towns of Sälen and Mora—is now the basis for one of the oldest, longest, and largest cross-country skiing races in the world: Vasaloppet. Staged every March in central Sweden, it still runs 56 miles (90 km), and features over 15,000 skiers in the main event, plus many thousands more in the subsidiary races for those who wish to attempt a shorter distance. It was first held in 1922 and, apart from a couple of cancellations, has taken place annually ever since.

Jörgen Brink won the race three times in the early 2010s, and, at the time of writing, holds the record-winning time of three hours and 38 minutes. Only 10 of the previous winners finished in under four hours. Many professional skiers consider the Vasaloppet more important than World Championship or Olympic cross-country ski races, and it is a dream to cross the finish in first place. "The absolute top of my skiing career," is how Brink described it.

RIGHT: Vasaloppet has become so popular with cross-country skiers it has also spawned sister races in Finland, the US, Canada, Japan, and China

RED BULL X-ALPS

DISCIPLINE:
PARAGLIDING AND MOUNTAIN RUNNING

LOCATION:
SALZBURG, AUSTRIA TO MONACO

TOUGHNESS FACTOR:
✘✘✘✘✘✘✘✘ ✘ ✘

POTENTIAL HAZARDS:
PARAGLIDER CRASH, MOUNTAIN FALL

WWW.REDBULLXALPS.COM

"Above me is the clearest blue Alpine sky I've ever seen in my life. 2,500 meters below me is some of the most barren mountain terrain in Europe. Keeping me suspended precariously between the two is just 24 square meters of canvas and a harness barely bigger than my arse."

47° 48' 34.16" N, 13° 3' 18.04" E

"YOU NEED A COOL HEAD TO REGAIN CONTROL BEFORE YOU LOSE TOO MUCH HEIGHT OR ENTER FREEFALL"

This was British paraglider Aidan Toase describing his time competing in the Red Bull X-Alps—a 528-mile (850-km) paragliding and mountain-running race from Austria to Monaco, the route of which snakes westward along the backbone of the Alps, across the continent's wildest peaks and glaciers.

It takes place every two years and the rules are simple: using GPS to navigate, competitors must travel either by gliding (when the conditions are right) or on foot, carrying their paraglider. Along the route there are checkpoints. Overnight rest is obligatory. A one-person support team, with a vehicle, is permitted. In Toase's case, his support team was his girlfriend. "Not only was I armed with some of the finest equipment available—a paraglider and harness, GPS, barometer, mobile phone, emergency flares, emergency parachute, boots, four pairs of trainers, jackets, fleeces, helmet—but I also had the most wonderful support team in the form of my girlfriend.

She drove the van, organized the map reading, cooked all the meals, topped me up with energy drinks (I was burning up to 10,000 calories a day), and kept tabs on the weather. Her input was essential."

Paragliders use thermal updrafts to get airborne. Skillful gliders can surf the thermals like birds, gliding up and down between them, reaching speeds of 40 mph (64 km/h) and sometimes traveling up to 100 miles (160 km) in a single flight. "There are so many variables in paragliding," Toase explains. "Not only do you control direction with your hands on the brake lines, and by leaning from side-to-side, but you alter speed by pushing down on the speed bar with your legs. Then you have to watch constantly for thermals. A paraglider is basically just a huge canvas kite. Unlike other aircraft, if you hit turbulence, the wing can collapse. You need a cool head to regain control before you lose too much height or enter freefall. Make a mistake and the wing can cravat (tie itself in a knot like a tie), in which case you'll need to use your back-up parachute. It's at low

ABOVE: The start point for the race is Salzburg, where 33 teams set off on this epic journey

altitudes that you need to be most careful. If the wing collapses you may hit the ground before you have time to react."

At one point during his race, Toase caught a thermal rising out of a valley. "But what a thermal!" he remembers. "Suddenly, from having been dropping like a stone, I found myself catapulted up at seven meters a second... right toward what looked like a storm brewing." No paraglider wants to get caught up in a thunderstorm. As Toase explains, "You could end up being sucked up to 10,000 meters in a few seconds, where anything could happen. You'd be at the total mercy of the elements." He couldn't risk this so he folded the wing of his paraglider, using a technique known as a "big ears," and descended out of trouble. Then he re-inflated his wing fully and glided away.

Swiss paraglider Christian Maurer is a multiple X-Alps winner. Incredibly, he once completed the course in less than seven days. "I really feel alive when I'm flying," he says. "I love being alone up in the air with my paraglider, feeling the power of nature." But Maurer admits he could never have won the X-Alps without the help of his support partner Thomas Theurillat. "I needed a partner to push me but sometimes also to slow me down," he says. "He was really important to me. He was my motivator, he was my coach. But in the race, he was also our cook, my mountain guide, and my nurse."

ABOVE: The tranquil setting of the Alps belies the dangers faced by the paragliders. One false move during a descent and it's curtains

VENDÉE GLOBE

DISCIPLINE:
SAILING

LOCATION:
LES SABLES-D'OLONNE, FRANCE AND AROUND THE WORLD

TOUGHNESS FACTOR:
✖✖✖✖✖✖✖✖✖✖

POTENTIAL HAZARDS:
CAPSIZING, DROWNING, SHIPWRECK

WWW.VENDEEGLOBE.ORG

You'll need a boat for this one. And not just any old boat. To have any chance of completing the Vendée Globe, indisputably the world's toughest sailing race, you're going to need a top-of-the-range ocean-faring yacht that will serve you faithfully on your solo, non-stop circumnavigation of the planet. The race starts and finishes in the town of Les Sables-d'Olonne, on France's west coast.

ABOVE: The ability to navigate successfully in all types of weather is the key to victory

"ERRATIC WINDS, VIOLENT THUNDERSTORMS, SOMETIMES TORRENTIAL RAIN"

From there, intrepid navigators head west to east around the Earth, via the Cape of Good Hope on the southern tip of Africa, Cape Leeuwin on the southwestern tip of Australia, and Cape Horn on the southern tip of South America. Although they are allowed to anchor during their circumnavigation, competitors cannot stop in ports, nor receive any outside assistance. It's a lonely challenge, that's for sure.

The first big test is the notorious Doldrums, the area of low pressure that has caused sailors problems for centuries. "Erratic winds, violent thunderstorms, sometimes torrential rain," warns the race organizer. "Going through the Doldrums is a bit like getting a lottery ticket." Once around the Cape of Good Hope, yachtsmen then face a long, daunting ordeal across the Indian and Southern Oceans, with their strong westerly winds known as the Roaring Forties and the Furious Fifties. The organizers describe what's in store: "Low light, dangerous seas, violent winds, a cold, wet environment. The change is a shock and can weigh heavily on [the sailors'] feelings. It is a question of getting the right mixture: knowing how to sail quickly without pushing the boat too hard. And above all, knowing how to survive."

Before rounding Cape Horn, there's a serious risk of collision with icebergs. As the organizers explain: "This means a stressful watch for the yachtsmen who, although able to detect the larger icebergs on the radar, cannot spot growlers—small blocks of drifting ice, which are sometimes less than a meter above the surface of the water, but which can weigh 30 or 40 tonnes. There is a permanent risk of collision and the hours spent on deck trying to detect the danger add to the tiredness." Finally, competitors have to deal with the violent Pampero (gales) along the South American coast, before negotiating the Doldrums for a second time.

The race was set up in 1989 by Frenchman Philippe Jeantot. He came fourth in his inaugural race behind Titouan Lamazou, the very first winner, who finished in 109 days. (Today's champions are closer to 80 days.) Since then, dozens of talented sailors have completed the race. Dozens more have failed to finish.

One of the latter was British sailor Tony Bullimore who, in the 1996 Vendée Globe, capsized in the Southern Ocean and survived for four days in an air pocket beneath the upturned hull of his yacht. His only food was a single bar of chocolate. Bullimore had pretty much resigned himself to a watery grave when suddenly, out of the blue, he heard banging on the side of the boat. Realizing it must be a rescue attempt, he leapt from his air pocket into the sea and swam out from beneath his yacht. There to greet him were servicemen from the Australian navy and air force.

"I started shouting: 'I'm coming, I'm coming!'" Bullimore recalled in an interview with the **Guardian** newspaper. "It took a few seconds to get from one end of the boat to the other. Then I took a few deep breaths and I dived out of the boat. When I saw the ship standing there and the plane going overhead and a couple of guys peering over the top of the upturned hull, it was heaven, absolute heaven."

Bullimore explained how close he was to giving up on life. "I really never thought I would reach that far. I was starting to look back over my life and was thinking, 'Well, I've had a good life, I've done most of the things I had wanted to.' If I was picking words to describe it, it would be a miracle; an absolute miracle."

PATROUILLE DES GLACIERS

DISCIPLINE:
SKI MOUNTAINEERING AND SKI TOURING

LOCATION:
ZERMATT TO VERBIER, SWITZERLAND

TOUGHNESS FACTOR:
✖✖✖✖✖✖✖ ✖ ✖ ✖

POTENTIAL HAZARDS:
AVALANCHES, CREVASSE FALLS, EXPOSURE

WWW.PDG.CH

You know things are serious when the army is involved. The Patrouille des Glaciers is a ski-touring race staged by the Swiss military—with both soldiers and civilians taking part. Held every two years in late April and early May in southwest Switzerland, the event pitches three-person teams (or patrols) against one another in a brutal test of ski touring, backcountry skiing, and basic mountain climbing. Due to the short sections of mountain climbing, the race is sometimes described as a ski-mountaineering, rather than a ski-touring, event.

46° 5' 45.87" N, 7° 13' 43.95" E

"SKI-TOUR RACING MAKES YOU HAPPY, IRRESPECTIVE OF WHAT PLACE YOU FINISH"

Each patrol is equipped with specialist equipment, such as skis, ice axes, a compass, an altimeter, climbing harnesses, ropes, snow shovels, headlamps, and an avalanche transceiver, plus all the normal cold weather gear one would expect when freezing one's proverbials off at the top of an Alpine peak in a snowstorm.

On some sections the competitors find themselves speed-hiking in trainers, carrying skis and other equipment on their backs; for other sections they might be ski touring uphill using climbing skins, or skiing fast downhill without. The three team members are often roped together in case of crevasse falls. So popular is the race that there are now two routes on offer: 32 miles (53 km) from Zermatt to Verbier, or 16 miles (26 km) from Arolla to Verbier.

The first Patrouille des Glaciers took place during World War II to test Swiss soldiers' "physical preparedness and technical proficiency in harsh alpine terrain." In 1949 it was cancelled after three soldiers died when they tumbled into a crevasse on the Mont Miné Glacier, and it wasn't revived until 1984.

German-born Benedikt Böhm is an accomplished Patrouille des Glaciers competitor: "Ski-tour racing makes you happy, irrespective of what place you finish," he says. "I have yet to see an unhappy runner cross the finish line. It's this

combination of a slow, easy ascent and rapid descent that grips you. The feeling of entering Verbier after all the strain, exhaustion, and wonderful experiences, and the sight of the many happy faces radiating 'I did it,' is simply awesome."

ABOVE: Competitors race in three-person teams, or patrols

SPARTATHLON

DISCIPLINE:
ROAD RUNNING

LOCATION:
ATHENS TO SPARTA, GREECE

TOUGHNESS FACTOR:
✖✖✖✖✖✖✖

POTENTIAL HAZARDS:
DEHYDRATION, HALLUCINATIONS

WWW.SPARTATHLON.GR

Every runner worth his salt is familiar with the famous legend of Pheidippides, the Ancient Greek messenger whose 26.2-mile (42-km) run from Marathon to Athens to deliver news of the Greeks' victory over the Persians (at the Battle of Marathon in 490BC) is said to have inspired the modern marathon race. Unfortunately, the poor chap promptly died after delivering his message.

37° 4' 28.06" N, 22° 25' 48.95" E

Less known is the even more awe-inspiring run that Pheidippides is supposed to have made in the run-up to that historic battle. With Persian forces advancing on Athens, he was dispatched 153 miles (246 km) to Sparta to request reinforcements. After running through the night, he arrived there the following day. Unfortunately, the Spartans refused to help, so Pheidippides turned around and ran back to Athens. (No wonder he died after the battle.) On the way back, Pan, the Greek god of nature, is said to have appeared in a vision to Pheidippides. Legend has it Pan later helped the Athenians defeat the Persians.

Fast-forward two-and-a-half centuries to the 1980s, and a British Royal Air Force officer, Wing Commander John Foden, and his RAF chums decided to test whether it was really possible to run 153 miles (246 km) in a day and a half. Sure enough, they did it. Foden himself took around 36 hours.

Ever since then, an annual ultramarathon has been staged over the same distance, during the month of September—the same month Pheidippides supposedly made his epic run. And just like poor Pheidippides, the competitors have to run through the night.

Forty-five runners entered the first Spartathlon in 1983. Today over 200 runners take part, the winners finishing in closer to 20 hours than 30. Here's how the race organizers describe the ordeal they put their runners through: "The Spartathlon runs over rough tracks and muddy paths (often it rains during the race), crosses vineyards and olive groves, climbs steep hillsides and, most challenging of all, takes the runners on the 1,200 meter ascent and descent of Mount Parthenio, in the dead of night. This is the mountain, covered with rocks and bushes, on which it is said Pheidippides met the god Pan."

Ultramarathon runners push their bodies so hard and for so long that many of them start to hallucinate. It's possible that Pheidippides' vision of Pan was, in reality, one such hallucination brought on by fatigue and sleep deprivation.

American ultramarathoner Scott Jurek won the Spartathlon three times in the 2000s. In his biography **Eat & Run: My Unlikely Journey to Ultramarathon Greatness**, he explains how he started hallucinating in the closing stages of the race: "The last 30 miles of the race follow a narrow two-lane highway straight into Sparta," he writes. "I had never felt so tired. Several times I found myself dozing off as I ran uphill. I slapped my face to make sure I stayed awake. Then I saw the photographer, squatting on the double yellow line in the middle of the highway, snapping pictures of me as I approached. The closer I got, the more clearly I saw and the more he clicked until I was upon him, which is when he disappeared. It took me a moment to realize: he had never been there."

ABOVE: At the finish line is the statue of Leonidas, the warrior king of ancient Sparta. For many runners he represents the fighting spirit and determination needed to complete the race

VIRGIN MONEY LONDON MARATHON

DISCIPLINE:
RUNNING

LOCATION:
LONDON, ENGLAND

TOUGHNESS FACTOR:
✖ ✖ ✖ ✖ ✖ ✖ ✖ ✖ ✖ ✖

POTENTIAL HAZARDS:
**DEHYDRATION, BLISTERS,
INFLATABLE PIECES OF FRUIT**

WWW.VIRGINMONEYLONDON
MARATHON.COM

RIGHT: Buckingham Palace and The Mall
provide a suitably impressive backdrop to
the end of this incredibly popular challenge

Since it first started all the way back in 1981, the London Marathon has raised well over US$1 billion (£700 million) for charity. Close to a million runners have entered the event over the years, many of them—in a show of true British eccentricity—dressed as chickens, superheroes, astronauts, nurses, sailors, film characters, and inflatable pieces of fruit. One chap, Lloyd Scott, completed the 2002 race in a full-weight deep-sea diver's suit. It took him more than five days to reach the finish line.

The London Marathon course starts in the southeast of the capital and winds its way past many famous landmarks before ending close to Buckingham Palace. At the time of writing, the course record is held by Kenyan runner Wilson Kipsang who, in 2014, posted an unimaginably fast time of two hours, four minutes, and 29 seconds. The fastest woman is British long-distance runner Paula Radcliffe, completing the 2003 marathon in two hours, 15 minutes, and 25 seconds—a time which is also the current women's world record.

There are hundreds of marathon races held across the globe every year. The largest and best-known ones come under the banner of World Marathon Majors, with six races in all: Tokyo (February), Boston (April), London (April), Berlin (September), Chicago (October), and New York (November).

ÖTILLÖ

DISCIPLINE:
**OCEAN SWIMMING AND
CROSS-COUNTRY RUNNING**

LOCATION:
**STOCKHOLM ARCHIPELAGO,
SWEDEN**

TOUGHNESS FACTOR:
✗✗✗✗✗✗✗✗ ✗ ✗

POTENTIAL HAZARDS:
DROWNING, DEHYDRATION

WWW.OTILLO.SE

From the air, the 30,000 islands stretching across the Stockholm Archipelago look beautiful: jewels in the Baltic Sea. But when you're down at sea level, swimming between them, and running across them—dealing with rough seas, sharp rocks, and unforgiving terrain—you don't get an opportunity to observe their beauty. You're too busy gritting your teeth and blocking out the pain.

ABOVE: Navigating the hazardous rocky sections on the islands can be very dangerous, particularly when soaking wet

The Stockholm Archipelago in September (when the sea is at its warmest) is the setting for one of Sweden's toughest endurance races—ÖTILLÖ. ("Ö till Ö" is Swedish for "island to island".) The annual event sees teams of two swimming for a total of 6 miles (10 km) and running for a total of 40 miles (65 km), but with many transitions between the two disciplines. The course starts in Sandhamn and finishes, 26 islands later, on Utö. Carrying their running and swimming gear with them, competitors have to enter and exit the water a total of 50 times before they reach the finish line, cruelly preventing them from ever getting into any real rhythm. The swims range in length from just over 100 yards (100 m) to nearly 2,000 yards (1,780 m); the runs from 75 yards (70 m) to over 12 miles (19 km). Teammates must remain together at all times—on land they are disqualified if they stray more than 328 ft (100 m) apart, while in the water they must stay within 32 ft (10 m) of each other. Equipment is crucial, so most competitors both swim and run in cut-off triathlon wetsuits and running shoes, and you obviously need to be proficient at transitions. This race is considered the unofficial World Championship of swim-run racing.

It all started back in 2002 and, like all the best ideas, came about thanks to a drunken bet down the local pub. Anders Malm, the owner of the hotel that stands at the finish line of the ÖTILLÖ, challenged some of his friends to race him to the hotel that now stands at the starting line. The team of two that arrived last would have to pay for everybody else's drinks, dinner, and accommodation. By 2006 the race had grown to 11 teams. The latest edition saw well over 100 teams taking part.

"The elements on the course are unforgiving with harsh terrain and cold waters often with high waves," says Björn Englund who, at the time of writing, holds the course record, having completed the event in a very respectable time of eight hours and 35 minutes. New Zealander Penny Comins agrees. When she completed the race in 2013 she found the transitions from sea onto land the toughest aspect of the race. "As the waves rushed up the rock face, crashing me against them and then sucking me out as quickly as they had compressed me, I was more worried about my life than representing my country," she wrote in her blog. "Drawing on my rock-climbing lessons at school, I looked for finger holds and pulled up on the wave, scrambling with hand paddles flailing around my wrists and my pool buoy trying to separate my legs." Multiple ÖTILLÖ champion Jonas Colting is a bit more blasé when discussing the event. "The Baltic Sea is brackish water," he told **Outside** magazine. "There are no jellyfish. Basically, we don't have anything that is scary in Sweden. It's like Disney World here. It's a great mix between highs and lows. You'll be tired and frustrated from the terrain, then you reach a point on an island where it's really beautiful and tranquil."

ABOVE: There are so many islands that competitors enter and exit the water 50 times

THE SUP 11-CITY TOUR

The labyrinthine network of canals that sprawls across the Dutch region of Friesland is the perfect venue for the world's longest stand-up paddle surfing race—the SUP 11-City Tour.

"THAT'S WHEN YOU HIT THE WALL. YOU'RE LIKE 'OH S**T!'"

DISCIPLINE:
STAND-UP PADDLE SURFING

LOCATION:
FRIESLAND, NETHERLANDS

TOUGHNESS FACTOR:
✖ ✖ ✖ ✖ ✖ ✖ ✖ ✖ ✖ ✖

POTENTIAL HAZARDS:
CRAMP

WWW.SUP11CITYTOUR.COM

ABOVE: After paddling for over five days, the sense of relief is clearly evident on any finisher's face

In all, 136 miles (220 km) have to be paddled, over five day-long stages, starting and finishing in the town of Leeuwarden, the region's capital. The course is loosely based on an old ice-skating path that farmers once used to get around in winter. Set up by Dutchwoman Ann-Marie Reichman, the race has been going since 2009.

At the time of writing, Chilean stand-up paddler Arnaud Frennet holds the race record of 26 hours and 20 minutes. "When your mind and your body are totally connected, you get into a hypnotic state, and then you feel you're flying in the water," he said of his experience. "That's the best feeling. It can be a 26-hour or 30-hour race and then, at the end, it's weird—it's like it's only half an hour. I was trying to maintain that state somehow but at some point it can just go. That's when you hit the wall. You're like 'Oh s**t!'"

THE HAUTE ROUTE

DISCIPLINE:
SKI TOURING

LOCATION:
**CHAMONIX, FRANCE TO
ZERMATT, SWITZERLAND**

TOUGHNESS FACTOR:
✗✗✗✗✗✗✗✗ ✗ ✗

POTENTIAL HAZARDS:
**AVALANCHES, CREVASSE FALLS,
EXPOSURE**

This is arguably the most famous ski tour in the world. The Haute Route–around 112 miles (180 km) from Chamonix in France to Zermatt in Switzerland–was first completed in 1911 and, since then, has cemented its place on the bucket list of every ski tourer. They call it the "Queen of the Alps."

BELOW: Adventurers have being tackling the Haute Route for over 100 years

Ski touring involves crossing snowy mountain ranges by skiing up the inclines using climbing skins or ski crampons (to grip the snow), and then skiing down the inclines as on normal skis. For the Haute Route, skiers twist their way through the highest peaks of the Alps, starting near Mont Blanc and finishing near the Matterhorn, spending their nights in mountain huts. Really hardcore ski tourers spice up their challenge by ascending some of the mountain summits along the way. "Often you reach the huts in total whiteout conditions [using your] GPS," explains mountain guide Paolo Tombini. "As everyone knows, ambling about on a glacier in poor weather isn't the best of fun." At the time of writing, the record for the Haute Route Ski Tour is held by French gendarme and mountain guide Lionel Claudepierre, who completed the course in 18 hours and 5 minutes.

Not everyone follows the original Haute Route—there are other routes available in the area. In summertime, hikers follow a similar route on foot, taking advantage of the stunning landscape, just with less snow.

ABOVE: Competitors climb using crampons or climbing skins, then descend on normal skis

BELOW: L'Etape du Tour is one of the most popular and celebrated cyclosportives in the world

L'ETAPE DU TOUR

The Tour de France is responsible for many things. Shaved legs and tight Lycra spring to mind, for instance, as does the downfall of Lance Armstrong and that supporter who always dresses up as the Devil. Another repercussion is one of the world's most famous amateur road cycling events known as L'Etape du Tour.

Essentially, L'Etape gives us mere mortals the opportunity to ride an official stage of the Tour de France. First held in the early 1990s, it normally takes place on a rest day during the professional race and always includes some of the vicious *hors catégorie* (beyond categorization) climbs that have provided the backdrop for some of the Tour's most celebrated stages. Each year thousands of cyclists get involved, taking advantage of the closed public roads, and the chance to connect with the sport's most iconic event.

DISCIPLINE:
ROAD CYCLING

LOCATION:
FRANCE

TOUGHNESS FACTOR:
✕✕✕✕✕✕✕✕✕

POTENTIAL HAZARDS:
ROAD RASH, ALTITUDE SICKNESS, BONKING

WWW.LETAPEDUTOUR.COM

46° 13' 39.50" N, 2° 12' 49.50" E

PARIS-ROUBAIX CHALLENGE

The cobbles! Oh God! The cobbles! Mention the two words "Paris" and "Roubaix" to any seasoned road cyclist and his whole body will start to shake as he considers a race widely regarded as the toughest in professional cycling. The route of the annual Paris-Roubaix, one of Europe's, nay the world's, most infamous one-day bike races, is legendary for its bone-shaking, frame-wobbling cobbles, or pavés. They call it the "Queen of the Classics." Or the "Hell of the North."

DISCIPLINE:
ROAD CYCLING

LOCATION:
BUSIGNY TO ROUBAIX, FRANCE

TOUGHNESS FACTOR:
✗✗✗✗✗ ✗ ✗ ✗

POTENTIAL HAZARDS:
ROAD RASH

WWW.SPORT.BE/PARISROUBAIX

For the amateurs, normally the day before the main event, there's a slightly shorter race—an amateur sportive, to be precise. Its current route runs 105 miles (170 km) from Busigny to Roubaix in the north of France. Like the pro race, it finishes at the famous Jean Stablinski velodrome. Like the pro race, it includes merciless cobbles that shake you until you can be shaken no more.

"We were all shocked by the severity of the cobbles, how much they sap your energy," explains Oli Laverack in **Outdoor Fitness** magazine. "As scores of us descend onto the cobbles, clouds of dust kick up. The best line is usually in the gutter or on the crown of the road." There are certain techniques that riders employ to combat the vicious cobbles (graded throughout the route according to their severity). Firstly, they attack them at speed; the correct tire pressure is crucial; slightly wider tires than normal absorb vibrations; most riders double-tape their handlebars and hold them lightly to cut down the vibrations; finally, they often use mountain bike SPD pedals and shoes so they can clip in and out more quickly on the cobbled sections.

Another treacherous element riders face is the weather. Even the briefest of rain showers render the cobbes dangerously slippery, meaning it's often not a case of if a rider will crash, but when.

BELOW: The famous pavés have been the undoing of some of the biggest names in pro cycling

THREE PEAKS CHALLENGE

Climb any of the UK's three most iconic mountains on midsummer's day and you're bound to bump into more than a few fast-moving hikers in the throes of what's known at the Three Peaks Challenge. It's an unofficial race against time—and the slowly fading daylight—to hike up and down the tallest mountains in Scotland (Ben Nevis at 4,409 ft/1,344 m), England (Scafell Pike at 3,209 ft/978 m), and Wales (Snowdon at 3,560 ft/1,085 m), one after the other.

DISCIPLINE:
HIKING, SCRAMBLING

LOCATION:
ACROSS THE UK

TOUGHNESS FACTOR:
✖ ✖ ✖ ✖ ✖ ✖ ✖ ✖ ✖

POTENTIAL HAZARDS:
FALLING ROCKS

WWW.THREEPEAKSCHALLENGE.UK

Participants normally impose a 24-hour time limit on the challenge, forcing them to speed-hike the mountain paths and rapidly drive the 462 miles (744 km) in between starting locations, obeying the local speed limits at all times, of course.

Even more intrepid hikers occasionally undertake what's known as the Five Peaks Challenge, adding the highest peak in Northern Ireland (Slieve Donard) and in the Irish Republic (Carrauntoohil) into the mix. (Your cut-off time is normally extended to 48 hours for this one.) There's even the Six Peaks Challenge, requiring a brief stop on the Isle of Man, in the middle of the Irish Sea, to ascend Snaefell.

In 2004, Irishman Ian McKeever set the world record for the Five Peaks Challenge, hiking up and down all five peaks in 16 hours and 16 minutes. Tragically, nine years later, he was killed by a lightning strike while climbing Mount Kilimanjaro.

Luke Gordon completed the Five Peaks Challenge in mid-June 2008, taking advantage of the longest days of the British summer. But he gave himself the more generous 48-hour time limit. He started off in the Irish city of Cork, hiring a rental car and knocking off the two Irish peaks before dumping the rental car and taking the ferry across the Irish Sea from Dublin to Anglesey. He speed-hiked up Snowdon and Scafell Pike, before completing his challenge with an ascent and descent of Ben Nevis, traveling between them in another rental car. He finished with just half an hour to go before his 48-hour cut-off time.

"I found the toughest challenge of all was getting my body warmed up for the ascents after spending so long in the car between peaks," he explains. "Your body inevitably stiffens up. And even in midsummer it can be pretty cold and pretty wet on some of the peaks. This is the British Isles, after all. By the time I reached my fifth and final peak—Ben Nevis, the tallest of them all—I really had to drag myself out of the warm car and psych myself up for the hike to the top." Gordon says the descents were tougher than the ascents because of the pressure it put on his knees. During the entire duration of the challenge, he snatched less than eight hours of sleep.

LEFT: Wales' tallest mountain, Snowdon, is the second highest of the Three Peaks

TOUR DE FORCE

Ever thought you're crazy enough to take on the entire 2,175 miles (3,500 km) or so of the Tour de France? A cycling event called the Tour de Force (that's Force, not France) lets you do just that—except you don't have to be professional-level to take part. The Tour de Force is more of a biking holiday than a bike race. That's provided your idea of a holiday is pedaling thousands of miles around France in the space of a few days, of course.

DISCIPLINE:
ROAD CYCLING

LOCATION:
ACROSS FRANCE

TOUGHNESS FACTOR:
✖ ✖ ✖ ✖ ✖ ✖ ✖ ✖ ✖

POTENTIAL HAZARDS:
COLLISIONS WITH CARS, ROAD RASH

WWW.TOURDEFORCE.ORG.UK

This is how it works. A week in advance of the real Tour de France, participants pedal all the stages (usually 21 in total) of the official race route—just a bit slower than the professionals do it. But like the pros, they also end their odyssey on Paris's Champs-Elysées. The organizers provide luggage transfer, accommodation, sustenance, and medical and mechanical support. Riders are expected to raise money for charity and be able to endure stages that can often be up to 135 miles (220 km) in length.

British rider Ian Greasby completed the event in 2014. "If Tour de Force taught me one thing, it's that I love my bike, with the freedom it provides, the simplicity and ruggedness of life that the bike and mountains offer in complete harmony," he wrote in his blog.

Greasby completed his Tour in 161 hours and eight minutes. By comparison, that year's pro race winner, Italy's Vincenzo Nibali, finished in 89 hours and 59 minutes. But as Greasby pointed out, with just a little bit of self-mockery, the pros had the benefit of closed roads for the entire route.

"We cycled further (to and from hotels etc.) and dealt with traffic lights, and traffic in general. We also took photos, ate food, rode all of the cobbled sections, and didn't ride in a peloton most of the way. I'd say this probably slowed us down by about 66 hours, or so... Therefore, by my calculations, and had we had closed roads... I wouldn't have won the 2014 Tour. But I wouldn't have come last either."

ABOVE: Twisting hairpin bends are a common occurrence during Alpine stages of the Tour

IRON BIKE

You need legs of iron. You need nerves of iron. You need lungs of iron. Your bike, however, is best if it's made of carbon fiber or some other such lightweight material. This race through the Italian Alps is 373 miles (600 km) long, with 88,580 ft (27,000 m) of climbing, so you don't want to be carrying any extra weight.

DISCIPLINE:
MOUNTAIN BIKING

LOCATION:
PIEDMONT, ITALY

TOUGHNESS FACTOR:
✖ ✖ ✖ ✖ ✖ ✖ ✖ ✖ ✖

POTENTIAL HAZARDS:
BIKE CRASHES, MOUNTAIN FALLS

WWW.IRONBIKE.IT

The route stretches across the Italian Alps, starting in Piedmont, and incorporates countless lung-busting climbs and hair-raising descents. British rider Matt Page came fifth in 2013. Here he describes one of the many pants-wetting downhill sections of the stage race. "Reaching the top, I set off flat out and into the first section, which was part of a downhill mountain-biking run, complete with big berms, doubles, drops, and loose corners. In the middle section there was some fantastic singletrack and just a few pedaling bits. The final section to the bottom was through a village, weaving along narrow streets, round a really fast, loose corner and a flat-out section to the finish line."

The race organizers describe their event as "the world's hardest mountain bike ride." Page says it definitely lives up to this reputation: "I don't think there is anything quite like it anywhere else. Despite being stupidly tough, it has enormous appeal and I love the racing and all the emotions that it gives. Nothing else I've ever ridden demands a more rounded rider or fitness. To be a finisher at Iron Bike is a tremendous achievement. Physically, I was spent. Mentally, stage three broke me. And every other day brought unique challenges within my mind to overcome."

THE RACE ORGANIZERS DESCRIBE THEIR EVENT AS "THE WORLD'S HARDEST MOUNTAIN BIKE RIDE"

CHAPTER 3

AFRICA AND ASIA

CAPE EPIC

DISCIPLINE:
MOUNTAIN BIKING

LOCATION:
WESTERN CAPE, SOUTH AFRICA

TOUGHNESS FACTOR:
✗✗✗✗✗✗✗✗ ✗ ✗

POTENTIAL HAZARDS:
**MOUNTAIN CRASHES,
SNAKEBITES, STINGING FLIES**

WWW.CAPE-EPIC.COM

It's not an exaggeration to say that the Cape Epic is mountain biking's Tour de France—except it's held in South Africa, and it's open to amateurs as well as professionals. Staged across the beautiful Western Cape region, it features teams of two bikers normally riding eight-day stages for around 500 miles (800 km) in all, normally with well over 52,000 ft (16,000 m) of climbing.

BELOW: Throughout the race, riders must remain close to their teammates—within two minutes—otherwise a one-hour penalty will be added to their overall time

Like the Tour de France, the route changes every year, and includes plenty of climbing. Unlike the Tour de France, riders have to negotiate dirt tracks, mountain paths, lush forest trails, bone-dry bush veld, and lots of twisting singletrack. There are some decidedly perilous descents, too, with lots of opportunity for wipeouts. The route designer's apt nickname is "Dr Evil."

Over 4,500 riders have so far completed the race since it first started in 2004. Just a handful of teams took part in the early days but, in recent years, thanks to major sponsors and excellent TV coverage, the event has grown enormously in popularity.

With two-person teams competing over such long distances, the camaraderie is obviously crucial in this race. Teammates are disqualified if they ever stray more than two minutes apart on three separate occasions. Kevin McCallum competed in the 2012 Cape Epic alongside teammate Jack Stroucken. The two men had never met before they embarked on the race, and were paired together by the race organizers. The experience of riding 500 miles (800 km) alongside each other under race conditions made them feel like best friends by the time they reached the closing stages.

"Tears welled, and I rode up ahead of Jack so he could not see them as they streamed down my cheeks," McCallum wrote in the official Cape Epic ride guide. "I drifted back and tried to tell him how wonderful he had been to me, how he had helped me at my lowest point and made me believe I could finish the race. Jack and I had never met before the Cape Epic... But it was a partnership that worked because of Jack's patience and strength and my desire to prove a lot of people wrong. One professional rider had bet his teammate 100 Rand I wouldn't finish. He lost."

And in case you were wondering whether the physical ordeal of 500 miles (800 km) takes its toll on the riders... well, you'd be right. It's not only the rugged terrain that leaves riders absolutely knackered, the blisteringly hot South African weather plays its part as well. Here's how virgin rider James Heraty described day three of his 2011 attempt at the race: "I'm scorched," he wrote in **Outdoor Fitness** magazine. "The sun is beating down hard and I'm fixated on the hypnotic rotation of my front wheel on the loose ground. I manage to stay tuned in to the regular shouts from my teammate, but the salt deposits on my shorts and the lack of power in my legs tell me I'm suffering dehydration."

Joyce Benade is a multiple Cape Epic finisher. "Don't focus on just one pain," she sensibly advises fellow competitors. "If your leg is sore, think about your shoulder that also hurts. Then think about your finger."

THE MONGOL DERBY

DISCIPLINE:
HORSE RIDING

LOCATION:
THE MONGOLIAN STEPPE

TOUGHNESS FACTOR:
✖✖✖✖✖✖✖ ✖ ✖ ✖

POTENTIAL HAZARDS:
**FALL FROM HORSE,
DEHYDRATION**

WWW.THEADVENTURISTS.COM
/MONGOL-DERBY

If Ghenghis Khan were still around, he'd win this race hands down. The Mongol Derby involves riding horseback for 620 miles (1,000 km) across the vast wilderness of the Mongolian Steppe—in stages, and on semi-feral horses. At night competitors stay either in nomad camps, or sleep rough beneath the stars.

47° 27' 1.39" N, 102° 43' 43.43" E

SO WHAT'S IT LIKE IN THE MONGOLIAN WILDERNESS WITH JUST A SEMI-FERAL HORSE FOR COMPANY?

"This is no guided tour, or pony trek," the organizers warn. "There is no marked course, no packed lunches, no shower block, no stabling. That's the whole point. It's just you, your team of horses, and 1,000 km of Mongolian wilderness."

The race route is based on an ancient postal network where messages were relayed across country on horseback, with riders refreshing their steeds at stations along the way. Just like those ancient postmen, Mongol Derby riders must be skilled equestrians. They need to know the art of bushcraft. ("A facility with knots, maps, and, in extremis, capturing a loose horse in a field three times the size of France, are all key skills," explains Katy Willings in **Adventure World** magazine.)

Since they spend up to 14 hours a day in the saddle, riders need to be very fit. They must also be light. Mongolian horses may be "fearless, wild, and unbelievably tough," but they're also small, meaning that riders, when fully dressed, cannot weigh more than 187 lb (85 kg). The only nod to modernity is a satellite tracker on each competitor so they don't spend weeks stumbling around barren, featureless plains, utterly lost.

ABOVE: Riders console each other after another hard day in the saddle

So what's it like in the Mongolian wilderness with just a semi-feral horse for company? "Almost everyone can expect to take a tumble along the way," Willings writes. "And dehydration and exposure slow a few folks down before they hit their stride and develop their appetite for mutton and fermented mare's milk—the staples on offer along the way." But, she says, there's a beauty in the barren desolation of the race route. "Getting lost in one of the most sparsely populated and luxury-free countries on earth, pitting yourself against innumerable hazards, and riding semi-wild and fairly feisty horses across all sorts of terrain, two days from the nearest hospital, appeals to a certain type of person."

Chris Maude, a former jump jockey from the UK, is one such person. In 2014 he finished joint second in the Mongol Derby. "The food was horrific," he told **Telegraph** journalist Marcus Armytage after finally crossing the finish line. "We slept in gers [yurts] which smell revolting. But, by day four, they smelt better than us. And we learned that Mongolians don't do privacy. If you go behind a bush, you find the whole village comes to have a look. I can't wait for a WC with a door on it." Sam Jones, a female mining operator from Australia, who won the Mongol Derby in 2014, called the race "the equine equivalent of climbing Everest."

ABOVE: Competitors have to ride semi-feral and very feisty horses

MARATHON DES SABLES

For camels, the Marathon des Sables—a 150-mile (240-km) foot race across some of the most desolate areas of southern Morocco's Sahara desert—is a walk in the park. For humans, it defies logic, turning the most hardy of ultramarathoners and adventurers into gibbering wrecks. Every year many competitors are forced to abandon. Discovery Channel once dubbed it "the toughest foot race on Earth."

DISCIPLINE:
RUNNING

LOCATION:
SAHARA DESERT, MOROCCO

TOUGHNESS FACTOR:
✖ ✖ ✖ ✖ ✖ ✖ ✖ ✖ ✖

POTENTIAL HAZARDS:
SUNSTROKE, DEHYDRATION, SANDSTORMS

WWW.MARATHONDESSABLES.CO.UK

Between the six different race stages (the longest being 51 miles/81 km), competitors must carry their own food (a minimum of 2,000 calories per day is recommended), basic equipment, and sleeping bag. At night they sleep in bivouac tents. During the day they face everything the desert throws at them, including vicious sandstorms. "Imagine yourself in the Sahara desert with nothing but rolling sand dunes for miles around," the organizers explain. "When you plow your feet through the sand, a fine dust kicks up. You can't feel the sweat dripping down your face because it's evaporating in the baking heat. Your lungs feel parched. Today's temperature is over 100°F. Part of your brain is screaming at you to stop, right now; to drop out of the race. But the other part of your brain is stronger." One competitor, whose brain is perhaps strongest of all, is Moroccan ultramarathoner Lahcen Ahansal,

who won the Marathon des Sables 10 times between 1997 and 2007. Brought up in a family of desert nomads, he knows the sands of the Sahara better than anyone. And he knows how infuriating it can be, trying to run (or often just march, on the double) on a constantly shifting surface that offers very little support. He knows that however much you protect your shoes, the particles of sand get into them and cause excruciatingly painful blisters. And he knows what it's like to become totally disorientated in the middle of a gruesome sandstorm.

The race organizers don't pull any punches when it comes to warning potential competitors of what to expect. They suggest that "at least 50 percent of your preparation" should go into battling the mental stress you will face. They sing the praises of concentrated food, and of attentive desert

navigation. They warn of midday temperatures as high as 120°F (50°C), and of the "six-legged, eight-legged, and no-legged" creepy-crawlies you are likely to meet.

Famous polar explorer Sir Ranulph Fiennes decided, at the ripe old age of 71, to try his hand at the Marathon des Sables in 2015. He agreed that it was the mental rather than the physical stress that weighed heaviest: "It's all about dealing with the wimpish voice which comes into your head saying 'Is it worth it? I think we'd better stop.' The ability to shut that voice up in your own head, and stop it tempting you, is very important."

RIGHT: A lone athlete struggles with the heat as he attempts to climb one more in a seemingly endless line of sand dunes

TRANS ATLAS MARATHON

Run this six-day ultramarathon (177 miles/285 km in stages across the High Atlas in Morocco), and you get to see some of North Africa's most stunning scenery. "Crossing Jbel Toubkal, North Africa's highest peak at 13,670 ft (4,167 m), the landscape is spectacular: snow-capped peaks contrast with lush valleys cultivated by Berber communities who have inhabited these areas for thousands of years," the organizers say.

DISCIPLINE:
CROSS-COUNTRY RUNNING

LOCATION:
ATLAS MOUNTAINS, MOROCCO

TOUGHNESS FACTOR:
✖ ✖ ✖ ✖ ✖ ✖ ✖ ✖ ✖

POTENTIAL HAZARDS:
DEHYDRATION, SUNSTROKE

WWW.BEYONDTHEULTIMATE.CO.UK

"Then there's the Toubkal National Park, the rich oases of the Draa Valley and the Dadès Gorges, and the volcanic Jbel Saghro massif, with its lunar-like landscape of plateaus and sharp peaks. The villages around this massif are relatively few—palm trees appear everywhere. Pomegranates, fig, and almond trees offer a magical spectacle. Jbel Saghro is also the home of the Ait Atta nomads, with their bedouin tents and their herds of goats."

It sounds amazing, which is just as well when you consider the punishing ordeal the athletes have to put themselves through in order to witness all of this. As well as the early summer heat and the altitude, they must also take on around 45,900 ft (14,000 m) of cumulative elevation. The daily stages range between 18 miles (30 km) and 37 miles (60 km). Runners carry their own day's supply of equipment, food, and drink.

The race is organized by two expert ultramarathon runners, brothers Lahcen and Mohamad Ahansal. Together they have won a total of 15 Marathon des Sables titles (see page 96). They were brought up in a nomadic family in the Sahara desert.

RIGHT: A runner crosses one of the deep valleys using a rope bridge

GREAT ETHIOPIAN RUN

DISCIPLINE:
ROAD RUNNING

LOCATION:
ADDIS ABABA, ETHIOPIA

TOUGHNESS FACTOR:
✖ ✖ ✖ ✖ ✖ ✖ ✖ ✖ ✖ ✖

POTENTIAL HAZARDS:
HEART ATTACK

WWW.ETHIOPIANRUN.ORG

They know how to run long-distance in Ethiopia. This is a country that has produced countless Olympic champions in 5000 meters, 10,000 meters, and the marathon. And this is the country that contains the Kalenjin tribe of the Great Rift Valley, members of which could, according to some statistics, outrun around 90 percent of the rest of the human race. So expect some strong competition if you take on the Great Ethiopian Run, a 6-mile (10-km) road running race that takes place every November in the Ethiopian capital Addis Ababa.

At 6 miles (10 km), it's not the distance that makes this race tough; rather it's the pace and the size of the field. Well over 37,000 runners enter nowadays, making it Africa's largest road running race. The world record for 10,000 meters (at the time of writing) is 26 minutes and 17 minutes. The Great Ethiopian Run has the disadvantage that it's staged on city streets at an altitude of 7,710 ft (2,350 m). Nevertheless, winners regularly post times under 30 minutes.

The race director (and winner of the inaugural race back in 2001) is Haile Gebrselassie, double gold medalist in the Olympic 10,000 meters and local legend.

ABOVE: Race director Haile Gebrselassie

COMRADES MARATHON

There are hundreds of ultramarathons staged across the globe every year. The Comrades Marathon, run annually in South Africa since 1921, claims to be the oldest and the biggest.

DISCIPLINE:
ROAD RUNNING

LOCATION:
DURBAN TO PIETERMARITZBURG, SOUTH AFRICA

TOUGHNESS FACTOR:
✖ ✖ ✖ ✖ ✖ ✖ ✖ ✖ ✖ ✖

POTENTIAL HAZARDS:
DEHYDRATION, HEAT EXHAUSTION

WWW.COMRADES.COM

ABOVE: Celebratory scenes as runners cross the finish line together

NOWADAYS, THE MARATHON IS SO POPULAR THAT THE FIELD HAS TO BE CAPPED AT 18,000 RUNNERS

It was set up by Vic Clapham, after he returned home at the end of the First World War, to commemorate his fallen comrades. Just 34 runners competed in the inaugural event. Nowadays, it's so popular that the field has to be capped at 18,000 runners. Over the years well over 300,000 runners have taken part. The asphalt route stretches 56 miles (89 km) between the cities of Durban and Pietermaritzburg, taking in five sets of hills. Every year the direction of the race switches.

Halfway along the race route is the Comrades Marathon Wall of Honor. "When the sun rose above the chill dawn air of Pietermaritzburg on 24 May 1921, few realised that the stage was set for the beginning of one of the world's toughest and most enduring road races," reads the dedication. "At the start were 34 determined men—the first members of an elite club of 'Comrades' dedicated to a common goal: running as fast as they could."

29° 51' 31.25" S, 31° 1' 18.62" E

YAK ATTACK

No one has yet been killed by a yak in this race, but there's always that possibility. The annual Yak Attack mountain bike stage race sees riders tackling a 248-mile (400-km) course across the Himalayas with an overall altitude gain of 39,370 ft (12,000 m), and a temperature range from 5°F (-15°C) to 86°F (30°C). At the highest point, competitors find themselves over 16,400 ft (5,000 m) above sea level. Helicopters are on standby to evacuate any riders who get into serious trouble.

DISCIPLINE:
MOUNTAIN BIKING

LOCATION:
THE HIMALAYAS, NEPAL

TOUGHNESS FACTOR:
✖✖✖✖✖✖✖✖✖

POTENTIAL HAZARDS:
BIKE CRASH, ALTITUDE SICKNESS

WWW.THEYAKATTACK.COM

British mountain biker Neil Cottam has completed the race several times without getting into too much trouble. Here's how he describes his experience: "Heat, cold, altitude, punishing climbs, dust, sand, rock, mud, river crossings, snow, ice, extreme winds, yaks, and the mighty Thorong La pass at 17,770 ft (5,416 m). The Yak Attack is rightly considered one of the toughest mountain bike stage races on Earth. It tests the mettle of the world's hardiest riders. It's an awesome experience that tests not just your ability to ride a mountain bike but your ability to survive everything that the Nepalese Himalayas can throw at you. This isn't your common or garden stage race.

Deprived of western comforts, international riders find themselves in a remote, but spectacular region. With minimal luxury, basic food and facilities, harsh, saddle-sore-inducing trails, the likelihood of stomach issues, and debilitating levels of oxygen in the higher stages, it is a true test for the adventurous rider."

ABOVE: Helicopters are on standby to evacuate any riders who get into serious trouble

GREAT WALL MARATHON

DISCIPLINE:
RUNNING

LOCATION:
TIANJIN PROVINCE, CHINA

TOUGHNESS FACTOR:
✘✘✘✘✘✗✗✗✗✗

POTENTIAL HAZARDS:
FALLING DOWN STEPS

WWW.GREAT-WALL-MARATHON.COM

There's a story that the Great Wall of China is the only human-built structure visible from space. That may or may not be true. What you certainly can't see from space are the thousands of runners who take part every year in the Great Wall Marathon, a 26-mile (42-km) race run partially along this huge, ancient frontier originally built to keep out the Mongol hordes.

40° 14' 19.40" N, 117° 26' 47.94" E

Most of the race takes place in the villages and countryside neighboring the wall. But it's when the runners are pushing themselves along the top of the wall that things get really tough. That's mainly thanks to the 5,164 steps—many of them very deep and very steep—they are forced to negotiate.

One 5-mile (8-km) section, in particular, sees runners clambering up and down thousands of non-stop steps, adding "an hour or two" onto the time that serious runners normally clock up on a flat marathon.

Heat takes its toll on competitors, too. "Part of the route passes through a dry river bed littered with huge boulders that become red hot under the merciless sun," says organizer Søren Rasmussen. "Running through it felt like being in a sauna and the place was soon nicknamed 'the Gobi Desert.'"

Rasmussen decided to protect the runners from the worst of the heat by moving the race start time forward. "This proved to benefit the fast runners, who made it home pretty quickly," he adds, "but did little for the laggards who had to pass through the area with the sun fully up."

Initially, Rasmussen and his colleagues weren't sure how tough to make the race. "Just how many climbs and hills would we able to include along a route that featured more than 5,000 steps?" they wondered. "What would it be like for runners if temperatures reached 40°C? Would people fall off the wall? Would they die?" Fortunately, no one has yet died.

ABOVE: A steep section of stairs proves too much for some competitors, sapping their energy and forcing

RICKSHAW RUN

DISCIPLINE:
DRIVING

LOCATION:
ACROSS INDIA

TOUGHNESS FACTOR:
✖ ✖ ✖ ✖

POTENTIAL HAZARDS:
**CAR CRASH, MECHANICAL
BREAKDOWN, DELHI BELLY**

WWW.THEADVENTURISTS.COM
/RICKSHAW-RUN

"A 3,500 km pan-Indian adventure in a seven-horsepower glorified lawnmower. The Rickshaw Run is easily the least sensible thing to do with two weeks." If it sounds crazy, then that's because it is. The Rickshaw Run pitches teams—driving those three-wheeled contraptions so loved by Indian taxi drivers—against each other in a race across the Indian sub-continent.

20° 35' 37.26" N, 78° 57' 46.37" E

"No set route, no back-up, no way of knowing if you're going to make it," the organizers helpfully warn anyone brave/crazy enough to cross one of the world's largest countries. "The only certainty is that you will get lost, you will get stuck, and you will break down. It's just you and your mates in a wholly unsuitable vehicle, traversing the sub-continent, enduring whatever sh*t the road throws at you."

There are currently three race routes on offer. The shortest one (1,553 miles/2,500 km) runs from the south of the country to the northwest. The second (1,678 miles/2,700 km) runs straight across the top of India from the northwest to the northeast. Then there's the big one: 2,175 miles (3,500 km) from the northeast of the country (a city called Shillong) right down to Kerala in the south. It's currently held every August.

Here's how the organizers describe the rickshaw vehicle you'll be racing in: "Essentially, it's not a very good idea. It's not very fast, it smells, it falls over when you go round corners, it breaks downs more often than an emo teenager, and a day's driving feels like you've been kicked up the ass by an elephant. But somehow all this makes them better." Don't say they didn't try to warn you.

ABOVE: Spectacular hairpin bends and twisting, turning roads keep the entrants on their toes

GOBI MARCH

The Gobi Desert takes no prisoners; 500,000 square miles (1,295,000 km²) of sand and rock with winter temperatures dropping to an average of -17°F (-27°C). This is not a part of the world you want to get lost in. For that reason, competitors in the annual Gobi March—a 155-mile (250-km), six-stage foot race across China's Xinjiang Province—need to keep their wits about them.

DISCIPLINE:
RUNNING, HIKING

LOCATION:
XINJIANG PROVINCE, CHINA

TOUGHNESS FACTOR:
✗ ✗ ✗ ✗ ✗ ✗ ✗ ✗ ✗

POTENTIAL HAZARDS:
EXPOSURE, DEHYDRATION

WWW.4DESERTS.COM/GOBIMARCH

Actually, it's not all as bad as it sounds. The Gobi March takes place in summer and skirts the edge of the desert, taking on grasslands and uplands as well as sandy terrain. The fastest finish time for the event at the time of writing—23 hours and 12 minutes—was clocked by Spanish runner, Vicente Garcia Beneito, in 2012.

The race was founded in honor of three female Christian missionaries who, at the beginning of the twentieth century, traveled the trade routes of the Gobi Desert bringing their religious messages to the weather-beaten locals. "In this trackless waste, where every restriction is removed and where you are beckoned and lured in all directions, one narrow way is the only road for you," wrote one of the missionaries, Mildred Cable. "In the great and terrible wilderness, push on with eyes blinded to the deluding mirage, your ears deaf to the call of the seducer, and your mind undiverted from the goal."

Chinese runner Zhou Zhijun has taken part in the Gobi March several times. "I feel more content in life," he says, thanks to his experience of this harsh desert terrain. "Things that are hard, and daily life challenges, are so small in comparison. All the unhappiness I've experienced in my life seems like nothing compared to the challenges of the race."

BELOW: Hikers cross the desert in the shadow of the stunning Tianshan Mountains

DUSI CANOE MARATHON

DISCIPLINE:
CANOEING

LOCATION:
**MSUNDUZI AND MGENI RIVERS,
SOUTH AFRICA**

TOUGHNESS FACTOR:
✖✖✖✖✖✖✖✖✖✖

POTENTIAL HAZARDS:
**BLACK MAMBA SNAKE BITES,
DROWNING, FLASH FLOODS,
POISONOUS TICKS**

WWW.DUSI.CO.ZA

When it comes to African paddling, this is the big one. Founded in 1951, the Dusi Canoe Marathon tests canoeists on the Msunduzi and Mgeni Rivers along a 75-mile (120-km) course in eastern South Africa. As many as two thousand competitors enter each year. Featuring one-person, two-person, and three-person canoes, it is held over three days in mid-February, to take advantage of South Africa's summer rainfalls.

27° 37' 14.00" S, 30° 40' 36.00" E

OVER THE YEARS THERE HAVE BEEN RARE CASES OF DROWNING

Temperatures can be pretty harsh, often topping 100°F (40°C) in the valley sections. There are lots of rapids, some rated grade 3 or above, as well as testing portage sections. Anyone with a fear of white water probably shouldn't dwell too long on the course map. There, in black and white, are river-section names likely to strike fear into even the most accomplished canoeists: Devil's Cauldron, Son of a Gun, The Cascades, Graveyard, Jaws... no wonder the organizers insist all competitors have previous race experience. Over the years there have been rare cases of drowning.

The first ever Dusi Canoe Marathon champion was Ian Player. In the inaugural race in 1951 he took six days eight hours to complete the course, the only paddler of the original eight starters to finish. Along the way he endured low rivers, flash floods, and a nighttime adder bite. The fact that today's top canoeists complete the course in under eight hours of total paddling proves how far the sport's technique and technology has advanced.

But the greatest Dusi champion of all must be Graeme Pope-Ellis. Born and raised on the banks of the Msunduzi River, he first competed in the race in 1965 at the age of 17. His first win was in 1972 and after that he earned a total of 15 Dusi victories in one-man and two-man canoes.

"Pope-Ellis was known for his wide knowledge of the river and his ability to sum up situations during the race, and, more often than not, make the correct decision that would give him the edge over the other paddlers," the organizers say in tribute to their champion. "He was a great runner and was an endurance paddler who might have battled in sprints but was the man for the job on the long portages that are critical to the outcome of the Dusi every year."

Tragically, Pope-Ellis died in a tractor accident in 2010.

ABOVE: The high-grade rapids claim another victim

CHAPTER 4

SOUTH AMERICA, OCEANIA, AND BEYOND

THE DAKAR RALLY

DISCIPLINE:
OFF-ROAD RALLY DRIVING, MOTORCYCLING, TRUCK DRIVING, AND QUAD BIKING

LOCATION:
ARGENTINA, BOLIVIA, AND CHILE, SOUTH AMERICA

TOUGHNESS FACTOR:
✖ ✖ ✖ ✖ ✖

POTENTIAL HAZARDS:
MOTORING CRASHES

WWW.DAKAR.COM

Fatal crashes, spectators killed, terrorism, and extreme desert conditions...the Dakar Rally used to submit drivers to physical and psychological tests more brutal than in any other motor race on Earth. So brutal, in fact, that back in 2009 the race was moved from its original location, in Europe and North Africa, halfway across the world to South America. The course now runs mainly through Argentina and Chile.

24° 46' 58.56" S, 65° 24' 43.76" W

AMATEUR DRIVERS GET TO COMPETE ALONGSIDE PROFESSIONALS... ON THE SAME COURSE. IT'S ONE OF THE VERY FEW MOTOR RACES WHERE THIS IS THE CASE

It was for reasons of security—that of both the drivers and the spectators—that the race was relocated. Close to 30 competitors have died since the event first started in 1979. Much more controversial are the bystander deaths that have occurred—more than 40 in all—ranging from spectators hit by vehicles, to accidents among the support crew, and unwary pedestrians wandering onto the public roads used for the course.

Such a high-profile race has attracted criminals, too. One year around 50 drivers were ambushed by armed robbers, and dispossessed of vehicles, money, and fuel. As the gang made off with its booty, its leader was heard shouting: "See you next year!"

Terrorism has also reared its ugly head. In 2008 an armed group with links to Al Qaeda threatened to disrupt the event as it passed through Mauritania. The race was cancelled and relocated to South America in 2009.

Nonetheless, the basic format of the rally remains the same. The sport entails long-distance, mainly off-road rally racing (or rally raid, to use the technical term). In the Dakar

Rally there are four categories—cars, motorbikes, trucks, and quads. Competitors must negotiate all types of terrain, ranging from grassland and rocks to sandy desert. Around 80 percent of drivers are amateur. At first there were fears the switch in continents might undermine the event's enormous appeal. Quite the opposite, says Stéphane Peterhansel, the most successful driver in Dakar Rally history, winner five times in the car category and six in the motorcycle.

"The change of continent has given the rally a second life," the Frenchman explains in **Populous** magazine. "Even if the philosophy has changed a bit, I think it has some fine years ahead. There are lots of other countries to discover."

However, he admits the atmosphere of the rally has changed since its shift to the New World. "In Africa there was more a spirit of adventure. You were in areas where no one lived, in the desert for hundreds of kilometers. Now, civilization is never far away and spectators are always around. These are real fans of motor sport who come to cheer the drivers on. It's more a race of speed, less an adventure."

But perhaps the ultimate appeal of the Dakar Rally—and an element that the continental shift hasn't changed in the slightest—is the fact that amateur drivers get to compete alongside professionals at the same time, on the same course. It's one of the very few motor races where this is the case.

ABOVE: Around 80 percent of competitors are amateur drivers

CROCODILE TROPHY

When ex-Tour de France competitor Gerhard Schönbacher was researching the route for the first edition of this mountain bike stage race back in the mid-1990s, he couldn't initially think of an appropriate name. The Koala Trophy? The Kangaroo Challenge? It wasn't until he and his colleagues were camped in the outback of northern Australia that it came to him. One evening they spotted a sign that read: "Don't swim—crocodiles!" And so the Crocodile Trophy was born.

Two decades later and the race now features over 120 riders, all tackling a distance of 559 miles (900 km), with 55,770 ft (17,000 m) of elevation, spread out over nine stages. The terrain ranges from dense rainforest singletrack, jungle, and bushland to rough mining trails, river crossings, outback highways, and coastland paths. The modern race route crosses part of Queensland, from Cairns to Port Douglas. Riders race in teams of two, teams of three, or individually.

The 2014 winner was Australian-turned-Norwegian rider Greg Saw who completed the event in 26 hours and 53 minutes. Halfway through, he had a run-in with the vicious local flora known as the giant stinging tree. Stings from said tree have been known to kill dogs and horses that accidentally brush against them.

"I experienced a little bit of shock treatment via the stinging tree," Saw recalled after finishing the race. "It's like I've been tiptoeing through a minefield for nine days." Saw wisely used wax strips to remove the tree stings. "I guess nothing comes easy," he said stoically. "If it did, it probably wouldn't be so memorable."

DISCIPLINE:
MOUNTAIN BIKING

LOCATION:
CAIRNS TO PORT DOUGLAS, AUSTRALIA

TOUGHNESS FACTOR:
✗✗✗✗✗✗✗ ✗ ✗ ✗

POTENTIAL HAZARDS:
SNAKES, CROCODILES, STINGING TREES

WWW.CROCODILE-TROPHY.COM

ABOVE: Terrain includes jungle, bushland, outback trails, and, here, dense rainforest singletrack

SIMPSON DESERT BIKE CHALLENGE

DISCIPLINE:
MOUNTAIN BIKING

LOCATION:
PURNIE BORE TO BIRDSVILLE, AUSTRALIA

TOUGHNESS FACTOR:
✗✗✗✗✗✗✗✗ ✗ ✗

POTENTIAL HAZARDS:
DEHYDRATION, BIKE CRASH, SUNSTROKE

WWW.DESERTCHALLENGE.ORG

Purnie Bore and Birdsville aren't exactly major metropolis cities. In fact they're tiny little outposts in the driest region of the Australian outback. Population: a few kangaroos, and a handful of blokes with corks hanging off their hats. Perfect territory to set one of the world's toughest off-road races: the Simpson Desert Bike Challenge.

"...THERE ARE THREE THINGS YOU NEED TO GET THROUGH: BRAINS, BRAWN, AND BUTTOCKS OF STEEL"

Every September competitors have five days to cover the 360 miles (580 km) between Purnie Bore and Birdsville, west to east across the desert. The challenge is split into timed daily stages, with around 50 miles (80 km) in the morning and 31 miles (50 km) in the afternoon. It's a bleak, dry moonscape of red dunes, salt-crusted lakes, petrified forests, and vast stretches of grassland and scrub. There are no paved roads. In fact it's so inhospitable that during the Australian summer (December to March) the desert is often closed to visitors.

Much of the race route follows an old track built in the 1950s by an oil exploration company. Here's how the race organizers describe it: "The road has degraded over the years and conditions vary greatly from year to year. It is generally extremely corrugated, with stretches of deep sand and numerous wash-aways. The sand dunes are encountered in the first five stages, with the track flattening out as the race reaches the salt lakes on day three. The course then heads into big dune country and then some monumental climbs. Rain can transform the track overnight. It can be helpful by firming the sandy sections but can turn a smooth clay surface into a sticky bog that jams wheels solid with black goo in minutes."

Most competitors use mountain bikes with extra-thick tubeless tyres (at least four inches/ 10 cm wide) to combat the soft, sandy surfaces and the ubiquitous thorns that pepper the length of the track. Journalist Alan Keenleside described the race perfectly in **MBA** magazine. "As the challenge progresses, fatigue sets in. Hot foot, bum boils, and nerve damage all take their toll but the real battle is fought in the mind. There are three things you need to get through: brains, brawn, and buttocks of steel." Keenleside says speed isn't nearly as important as persistence. "With the heat, sand, and the wind, it's a race to survive," he writes. "12 km/h will do just fine, provided you can keep going." And only riders with the toughest of posteriors will survive. "The Simpson is ten times, in order of magnitude, harder on your backside than any other race in my experience," Keenleside writes. "I'd blistered one bum cheek and burst the other on the first day. By the fifth stage I was riding on two open sores. In the dry wind my sores scabbed over quickly and as I bent back over the bike they ripped open. The pain was excruciating." No wonder bikers call this race "Satan's Velodrome."

ABOVE: There is nowhere to hide from the blistering heat of the midday sun in these barren conditions

NULLABOOR LINKS

Depending on your handicap, 18 holes of golf can take anything from a couple of hours right up to an entire day. But there's one golf course—in the Australian outback—that will really test your endurance to the limit. It's called the Nullaboor Links. Stretching 848 miles (1,365 km) along southern Australia's desolate Eyre Highway, it's the longest golf course on the planet, by quite a margin.

DISCIPLINE:
GOLF, DRIVING

LOCATION:
KALGOORLIE TO CEDUNA, AUSTRALIA

TOUGHNESS FACTOR:
✖ ✖ ✖ ✖ ✖ ✖ ✖ ✖ ✖

POTENTIAL HAZARDS:
SNAKES, DINGOES

WWW.NULLARBORLINKS.COM

On paper it's just 18 holes, and par-72, but, even with the wind at your back, it takes a good week to complete. That's mainly because of the huge distances you'll need to travel between each hole—sometimes well over 60 miles (100 km). The course, ranging between Kalgoorlie in Western Australia to Ceduna in South Australia, can be played in either direction. You'll need more horsepower than a simple golf cart, however.

"Each hole includes a green and tee, and somewhat rugged outback-style natural terrain fairway," the owners explain. "The course provides a quintessential Australian experience."

You can say that again. Players are warned to look out for poisonous snakes, dingoes, and kangaroos (which can leap nearly 30 feet/9 meters, longer than many amateur golfers' tee shots). One hole claims to be home to Australia's largest population of southern hairy-nosed wombats. On another, there's a local crow that likes nothing better than stealing golf balls. "Try spraying smelly stuff on the balls," is the advice. Finally, keep an eye out for the enormous herds of feral camels that roam the outback and think nothing of chewing up all the grass on the greens.

ABOVE: A round on the Nullaboor Links is far from your average hack on your local course

THE ANTARCTIC ICE MARATHON

When you're running at the bottom of the world, it's all about keeping warm. To avoid frostbite, every part of the body, especially the extremities, must be well insulated. This means three layers on top, two layers on the legs, plus balaclava, face mask, goggles, hat, gloves, and mittens. "With the physical activity of running, the torso can sometimes overheat," says the race organizer. "So ventilation zips come in useful."

DISCIPLINE:
RUNNING

LOCATION:
UNION GLACIER CAMP, ANTARCTICA

TOUGHNESS FACTOR:
✗ ✗ ✗ ✗ ✗ ✗ ✗ ✗ ✗

POTENTIAL HAZARDS:
HYPOTHERMIA, FROSTBITE

WWW.ICEMARATHON.COM

"FOR THE LAST FIVE KM WE HAD TO RUN STRAIGHT INTO A 40-MPH WIND. SEVERAL TIMES I TURNED MY BACK AND RAN BACKWARDS"

Russian athlete Evgeniy Gorkov was the Antarctic Ice Marathon winner in 2005, posting a time of five hours and 10 minutes. "Physiologically, the most unpleasant environmental factor was the wind," he says. "Bitter winds in Antarctica flow from the pole to the edge of the continent, with few obstacles in their way. The course was a giant figure of eight, so we alternated between running into the wind and then away from it. For the last five km we had to run straight into a 40-mph wind. Several times I turned my back and ran backwards." Evgeniy hails from Moscow, so he's no stranger to freezing cold winter conditions. However, he didn't bank on the "mushy" running surface that makes the course even more challenging. "Running on snow is not very different from running on sand. It dissipates your push-off and saps your energy. After 26 miles you are at your wits' end."

The Antarctic Ice Marathon is staged near Union Glacier Camp, in the west of the continent, during the Antarctic summer. Nevertheless, don't be fooled by the time of year; the weather is far from balmy.

And if the ice marathon isn't enough for you, well there just so happens to be a second race from the same organizers, at the same venue. And at 62 miles (100 km), it's just a touch longer.

THE EVEREST MARATHON

DISCIPLINE:
MOUNTAIN RUNNING

LOCATION:
EVEREST BASE CAMP, NEPAL

TOUGHNESS FACTOR:
✗✗✗✗✗✗✗✗✗✗

POTENTIAL HAZARDS:
CLIFF FALLS, YAK ATTACKS, ALTITUDE SICKNESS

WWW.EVERESTMARATHON.ORG.UK

It's not the distance (a standard 26.2 miles/42 km) that makes the Everest Marathon such a lung-buster of a race, so much as the high altitude and rough terrain. Starting at the old Everest base camp, 17,000 ft (5,184 m) above sea level, runners have to negotiate ice, snow, scree, and rocks on a roller-coaster route to Namche Bazaar at 11,300 ft (3,446 m) above sea level.

27° 48' 24.75" N, 86° 42' 50.29" E

This being the Himalayas, nowhere is flat and runners are constantly ascending or descending, often precipitously. Hazards include dilapidated Indiana Jones-style suspension bridges over deep gorges, and aggressive yaks. "The yaks have huge horns and if you run below them you risk being knocked down a 1,000-foot cliff," warns organizer Diana Penny. "One Spanish gentleman finished the race with torn lycra

Kristina Madsen is a Danish runner who competed in the 2013 Everest Marathon. "One of the many challenges was starting the race at about minus 10°C while at the finish line it was plus 22°C," she told the race website. "When the marathon started I had three layers on: woolly underwear, a thin second layer, and a wind- and water-proof jacket. I wore good trail running shoes and a backpack with integrated drinking system.

The first kilometers were so cold I had to keep the drinking hose close to my body so the water would not freeze. In order to drink something I had to lift all the layers of my clothes. It was quite a challenge." So were the steep inclines. "Going uphill was really challenging because of low oxygen levels," she said. "My body started screaming for more oxygen during the hard work. It was really exhausting."

First staged in 1987, the Everest Marathon is a non-profit-making race that donates all proceeds to a charity for health and educational projects in rural Nepal. Another event—the Tenzing Hillary Everest Marathon—has been staged annually in the region since 2003.

"THE YAKS HAVE HUGE HORNS AND IF YOU RUN BELOW THEM YOU RISK BEING KNOCKED DOWN A 1,000-FOOT CLIFF"

shorts where he had been gored. He was from near Pamplona and should have known better." To enter, competitors must be experienced fell-runners. Altitude sickness can take its toll, as can dehydration, especially if, as Diana says, "you have recently suffered from a gastro-intestinal infection, which is a likely event when trekking in Nepal." Altitude sickness starts off by inflicting headaches, fatigue, and dizziness, but in severe cases it can lead to nausea, vomiting, hallucination, seizures, and even coma. Competitors are advised to train in a hyperbaric chamber or, better still, turn up at the race venue a few weeks early and acclimatize on site.

ABOVE: The marathon ends with a hair-raising descent into the village of Namche Bazaar

THE NORTH POLE MARATHON

Hungry polar bears, deep snow, bitter winds, and frostbiting temperatures of -22°F (-30°C)... If you like your home comforts, then perhaps the North Pole Marathon isn't for you. Although the course involves multiple laps, competitors have to run across constantly fluctuating ice floes so it's hard for them to measure just how well they are progressing.

DISCIPLINE:
RUNNING

LOCATION:
THE NORTH POLE

TOUGHNESS FACTOR:
✖✖✖✖✖✖ ✖ ✖ ✖

POTENTIAL HAZARDS:
POLAR BEARS, HYPOTHERMIA, FROSTBITE

WWW.NPMARATHON.COM

The winner might need anywhere from three and a half to five hours in all. One intrepid polar runner once had to shelter from the cold in his tent and took 20 hours to finish.

"The race occurs on a totally white landscape, so it's very easy to miscue distances," explains the event organizer Richard Donovan. "Each mile seems endless and much longer than a road marathon. It can be very psychologically demanding. The cold and tough terrain slow people down a lot, and it requires a lot of effort for many to finish."

And a lot of concentration, too. The route is well marked, but there is no solid ground at the North Pole. You're essentially running across huge slabs of ice. Head the wrong way and it's a very icy dip in the Arctic Ocean. "Each loop took us near the edge of a rift in the ice," says the 2006 winner Michael Collins, from Ireland, who completed the challenge in four hours and 28 minutes. "I feared somebody would fall into the sea. Where there is open ice, there are seals. And where there are seals, there are polar bears. This was always a potential threat."

Collins ran about 100 miles (160 km) a week in preparation for his race. To get accustomed to the cold, every morning he'd stand up to his thighs in two buckets of ice. "I'd read that explorers of old did this to get ready for the cold," he remembers. "The first week or so I was physically sick just standing in the ice. But by the time of the race I was used to it."

71° 42' 24.9696" N, 42° 36' 15.4908" W

LANCELIN OCEAN CLASSIC

Granted, they are able to harness the power of the wind. Nonetheless, you should never underestimate the sporting prowess of the competitors in the Lancelin Ocean Classic. It's billed as "the longest windsurfing and kitesurfing race in the world." Staged off the coast of Western Australia, north of Perth, it pitches more than 4,000 athletes across several disciplines. (Stand-up paddle boarding and jet skiing are included, too.)

DISCIPLINE:
WINDSURFING, KITESURFING

LOCATION:
LANCELIN, AUSTRALIA

TOUGHNESS FACTOR:
✗ ✗ ✗ ✗ ✗ ✗ ✗ ✗ ✗ ✗

POTENTIAL HAZARDS:
DROWNING

WWW.LANCELINOCEANCLASSIC.COM.AU

The headline event is the Ledge Point to Lancelin windsurfing marathon, which the **Guinness Book of Records** lists as the world's longest windsurf race. It's a 15-mile (25-km) journey north along the coastline that many consider one of the world's classic windsurfing events. Steve Allen is a multiple winner of this event, having won the race three times in a row between 2013 and 2015. At the time of writing his record time is just over 24 minutes, averaging a speed of around 37 mph (60 km/h).

ABOVE: The event includes the longest windsurfing race in the world

RIGHT: Racers can go for days without seeing any humans other than their teammates

PATAGONIAN EXPEDITION RACE

DISCIPLINE:
RUNNING, HIKING, MOUNTAIN BIKING, KAYAKING, CLIMBING

LOCATION:
SOUTHERN PATAGONIA, CHILE

TOUGHNESS FACTOR:
✗✗✗✗✗✗✗✗ ✗ ✗

POTENTIAL HAZARDS:
DROWNING, EXPOSURE, BROKEN LIMBS

WWW.PATAGONIANEXPEDITIONRACE.COM

Few of the races in this book offer competitors quite as much stunning scenery as the Patagonian Expedition Race, in southern Chile. The route changes every year, so nothing is set in stone. But at any point you might find yourself stumbling across ice fields, kayaking through the Straits of Magellan, scrambling up rocky crags, rope crossing torrential rivers, mountain biking across Tierra del Fuego, or rounding Cape Horn.

Staged every year since 2004, the race is open to teams of four. But here's the rub: competitors aren't told what the race route is until 24 hours before they're due to start. The only thing they can be sure of is that race organizers will have created a course that will see them having to negotiate mountains, forests, peat bogs, grasslands, rivers, lakes, fjords, icebergs, and glaciers, and that they will have to keep going for more than 370 miles (600 km). Most teams take between six and nine days to finish, sleeping for just a few hours every night and carrying all their own food, water, and supplies.

Nick Gracie is captain of Team adidas Terrex, which has won the race multiple times, their fastest completion in six days. "You're completely on your own as a team," he says when asked why the race is so tough. "You're really in the wilderness. It's not like you can call up an ambulance if you get into trouble."

Gracie goes on to describe the more dramatic elements of the race. "There are quite a few sketchy river crossings," he says. "You strip down naked, put all your clothes in a dry-bag, and then you swim across." With luck you get to put your clothes back on once you reach the other side.

The sea-kayaking sections were also fairly hairy for Gracie and his team. "The water was very rough and only five or six degrees C," he remembers. "So we wore dry-suits. But even then, if you fall in, you only have a few minutes before you need to get back in the boat. There are Antarctic winds there up to 100 mph." Gracie says the wind was especially gruesome on the hiking and mountain biking sections: "Sometimes the wind is so strong it's hard to walk against it. And if you're cycling on a gravel track, the wind picks up the gravel and throws it up at you. It's like being shot in the face by a shotgun."

ABOVE: A competitor leaps across a stream of glacial meltwater. One misplaced step and it's a bone-chilling dip in the freezing water below

JUNGLE MARATHON

"Can you cope with temperatures of 40 degrees C? Humidity of 99 percent? Primary jungle with a dense canopy covering and not a chink of daylight? Swamp crossings where anacondas lurk? River crossings with caiman and piranhas as companions?" The organizers of the Jungle Marathon, near the Brazilian town of Santarém, right in the depths of Amazonia, leave you in no doubt as to what tests runners must endure.

DISCIPLINE:
RUNNING

LOCATION:
SANTARÉM, BRAZIL

TOUGHNESS FACTOR:
✖✖✖✖✖✖✖ ✖ ✖

POTENTIAL HAZARDS:
SNAKES, INSECTS, HORNETS, JAGUARS, DEHYDRATION

WWW.JUNGLEMARATHON.COM

There are currently three distances on offer: a normal-length marathon, a four-stage 79-mile (127-km) race, and a six-stage 158-mile (254-km) race. With so many potential jungle hazards, the organizers ensure all runners are given a safety briefing by a "military jungle specialist" prior to the race. There are tips on jungle beasts (jaguars have been spotted), poisonous plants, and how not to get lost in the endless greenery of the Amazon rainforest.

There are checkpoints along the route where competitors can stock up on supplies and get medical attention. And if you needed proof of just how hot it can be in the jungle—one of the rules stipulates that it's automatic disqualification if you don't leave each checkpoint with at least 5 pints (2.5 liters) of water. There are also compulsory rests at certain checkpoints.

The organizers advise anyone taking part to get very used to running with wet feet: "Your feet will be saturated all day long, from both the climate and the numerous water crossings, so spend hours with wet feet during training and you are less likely to have problems during the race. In fact, if you can bear it, get into the shower fully clothed before you go out training (during hot months) to simulate being soaked through during the stages." Some runners have simulated jungle humidity by running on treadmills in saunas, or in hothouses at garden centers.

One British runner from the 2014 event gives a taste of what to expect. "I was descending a hill and heard people shrieking and screaming," recalls Amy Gasson, who finished eighth in the 170-mile (275-km) stage race in 63 hours and 33 minutes.

"A hornet's nest had somehow been disturbed and everyone was being stung. I ended up having seven stings including on my face. One man went into serious anaphylactic shock and had to have the medics rushed to him."

Gasson says the uneven terrain in the jungle is energy sapping: "We were met by hill after hill after hill after hill. They were relentless. They were practically vertical climbs and descents where we had to hold onto vines, trees, or anything safe we could get our hands on." She goes on to describe how, every evening, she had to remove her shoes carefully "to avoid taking any of the wet skin off with them" before popping blisters and taping up her feet. Then she was subjected to an all-over body check by the medical team for bloodsucking ticks. "I had five removed. Some people had three times as many." That's the jungle for you.

LEFT: All runners are given a safety briefing before the race by a "military jungle specialist"

SPEIGHT'S COAST TO COAST

New Zealand's South Island is long and thin. But not that thin. At its neck it's 151 miles (243 km) across. Here, every February, one of the country's most famous races takes place: the Coast to Coast.

THE WATER FLOWS SWIFTLY IN PLACES AND MIXES LONG CALM SECTIONS WITH RAPIDS UP TO GRADE TWO IN SIZE

DISCIPLINE:
RUNNING, ROAD CYCLING, KAYAKING

LOCATION:
KUMARA TO NEW BRIGHTON, NEW ZEALAND

TOUGHNESS FACTOR:
✖ ✖ ✖ ✖ ✖ ✖ ✖ ✖ ✖

POTENTIAL HAZARDS:
TWISTED ANKLES, CAPSIZED KAYAK, MOUNTAIN FALLS

WWW.COASTTOCOAST.CO.NZ

The action starts at Kumara Beach, on the west coast, and now finishes at New Brighton Beach, on the east coast. In between (on more recent editions, anyway) are six consecutive stages: a short run of 1.9 miles (3 km), a road biking section of 34 miles (55 km), a mountain run of 20 miles (33 km), biking 9 miles (15 km), kayaking 44 miles (70 km), and finally biking 42 miles (68 km).

The mountain run is a real test of endurance, featuring enormous boulders and fast-flowing rivers. "It's mainly off trail with the rocky riverbed often the only direct line up the valley," the organizers explain. "Multiple river crossings with frigid crystal-clear water, and an elevation gain of nearly 800 meters to Goat Pass and the start of the descent. With the very fastest athletes taking nearly three hours, the run is as much a test of coordination and strength as it is outright speed." The 44-mile (70-km) kayak section is a real classic, too. "For many it's both the highlight and the crux of the race," the organizers say. "The water flows swiftly in places and mixes long calm sections with rapids up to grade two in size."

The Coast to Coast (currently sponsored by New Zealand brewery Speight's, who offer competitors a well-earned beer or two at the finish) was first staged in 1983 with a field of just 79 competitors, which makes it one of the oldest multisport races in the world. Since the first edition the Coast to Coast has become legendary, and nowadays attracts fields of close to a thousand. The fittest athletes complete the race within one day. For the less extreme there is a two-day stage race with an overnight stay after the mountain run. Braden Currie won the 2015 event with a time of 11 hours and 27 minutes, taking home a prize purse of NZ$10,000. "It was tough. I went to some pretty dark places," he said afterward. With more than a little irony, Currie has been given the nickname of "Slug."

RIGHT: The Coast to Coast is a unique event in that it crosses an entire country in a day (or two, depending on how fit you are). Many active New Zealanders consider completing the race a rite of passage

BELOW: The route to Machu Picchu is popular with tourists and backpackers, who find it hard enough to walk the trail, let alone run it. To do so requires an intense physical effort as your lungs struggle to cope with the altitude and lack of oxygen

INCA TRAIL MARATHON

The Inca Trail up to Machu Picchu is arguably the world's most famous hiking route. Imagine, then, what a great backdrop it makes for a running race. That's what you get if you enter the Inca Trail Marathon: a 26-mile (42-km) race—starting at 8,000 ft (2,438 m) and ending at 13,800 ft (4,206 m)—that passes famous archeological sites on its way to the lost city of the Incas.

DISCIPLINE:
MOUNTAIN RUNNING

LOCATION:
CUSCO, PERU

TOUGHNESS FACTOR:
✖ ✖ ✖ ✖ ✖ ✖ ✖ ✖ ✖ ✖

POTENTIAL HAZARDS:
CLIFF FALLS, TWISTED ANKLES, BROKEN LIMBS

WWW.ANDESADVENTURES.COM

Richard Donovan won the race in the early 2000s, posting a time of five hours and 50 minutes—very impressive when you consider the elevation and the impact it has on the body. "The sheer altitude, coupled with the uneven and steep steps that characterize the Inca Trail, reduced my breathing to short, abrasive gasps," he wrote of his experience. "On many occasions, my hands were clasped fast to my thighs as I attempted to pull my legs up over the steps. Periodic stops to catch my breath became more frequent." Donovan was impressed by the local running talent. "It was both humbling and astonishing to see local porters keep pace at times, clad in old pairs of sandals and carrying heavy loads," he wrote.

When he finally reached the finish line he was blown away by the view. "Suddenly, the full grandeur of Machu Picchu, one of the world's most spectacular ruins, came into view. It was the most eye-catching sight I have ever seen."

BELOW: The lack of rainfall produces otherworldly conditions that resemble the sets of science-fiction movies

ATACAMA CROSSING

DISCIPLINE:
RUNNING AND HIKING

LOCATION:
ATACAMA DESERT, CHILE

TOUGHNESS FACTOR:
✗✗✗✗✗✗✗ ✗ ✗ ✗

POTENTIAL HAZARDS:
DEHYDRATION

WWW.4DESERTS.COM/ATACAMACROSSING

The Atacama Desert. Almost 50,000 square miles (129,500 km²) of sand, stones, and salt lakes between the Andes and the Pacific Ocean. Of all the deserts in the world, this is by far the driest. Some areas receive just 0.04 in (1 mm) of rain a year. There are weather stations here that have never recorded rain at all.

Perfect, then, for a seven-day, 155-mile (250-km), self-supported foot race. Don't forget your water bottles.

"Competitors will tackle sand dunes, gravel, loose rocks, hard-packed earth, and even waist-high grass during the event," the organizers warn. "This is in addition to the infamous salt flats that even the most dexterous of runners find nearly impossible to cross at full-speed."

Parts of the Atacama Desert are so barren and so dry that they resemble the surface of Mars. In fact, many filmmakers and space scientists have made use of this desert terrain precisely because of its extra-terrestrial properties. One competitor, Canadian Simon Melanson, describes it brilliantly in his race blog. "The salt flats gave way to a long sandy stretch of

PARTS OF THE ATACAMA DESERT ARE SO BARREN AND SO DRY THAT THEY RESEMBLE THE SURFACE OF MARS

undulating hills that breaded my shoes in burnt orange sand and made them feel heavy. Sand turned to dirt road and rocky plane that led to the Valley of the Moon. I have never seen such a haunting landscape. Giant orange and brown crusty structures popping out of the dry, cracked ground watching quietly as I ran past in the brutal midday sun. There was no shade to be found anywhere."

Another competitor, New Zealand's Inia Raumati, said the barren terrain made him

feel like "a cowboy in those old westerns where your horse is dead and you have no water, you're just waiting for the vultures to start circling."

The fastest finish time on any Atacama Crossing is 23 hours and 46 minutes, achieved by Spanish competitor Vicente Garcia Beneito.

The race organizers sum up the ordeal they impose on their victims as follows: "Life enhancing for all, life changing for many."

ABOVE: The beginning of the Long Crossing, a stage of 43–56 miles (70–90 km) that's around twice as long as any of the earlier four stages.

LA RUTA DE LOS CONQUISTADORES

DISCIPLINE:
MOUNTAIN BIKING

LOCATION:
HERRADURA TO LIMÓN, COSTA RICA

TOUGHNESS FACTOR:
✗ ✗ ✗ ✗ ✗ ✗ ✗ ✗ ✗

POTENTIAL HAZARDS:
JUNGLE BEASTS, MOUNTAIN CRASHES

WWW.ADVENTURERACE.COM

Costa Rica was a very different place in the sixteenth century when the Europeans first arrived. Thick jungle, untamed wilderness, thick jungle, and more thick jungle. Traveling anywhere required machetes, oodles of supplies, and great force of will. (Oh, and some spare machetes.)

LEFT: Riders cross a narrow gorge using a precarious old bridge

ABOVE: With a sheer drop on either side, sometimes it's safer to walk rather than ride

IS IT PHYSICALLY AND MENTALLY TESTING? YOU BET. PERHAPS NOT AS TESTING AS IT WAS IN THE SIXTEENTH CENTURY BUT IT'S NO AMBLE THROUGH THE PARK

In the 1560s, three Spanish conquistadores took years to complete the crossing of Costa Rica from the Pacific coast in the west to the Caribbean Sea in the east. Hacking their way through endless rainforest, traversing torrential rivers, and surmounting mountains and volcanoes, they constantly faced the wrath of jungle beasts, the unforgiving climate, and the understandably rather miffed indigenous population.

Intrigued by the story of those original conquistadores, a group of modern-day mountain bikers decided to replicate their medieval journey across the neck of Central America—but this time on two wheels. They set off in 1993, led by a very accomplished biker, Roman Urbina. Thanks to the existence of roads and tracks, their modern-day route was obviously a lot easier than that of the conquistadores. Nonetheless it was both challenging and inspiring. "Roman emerged more convinced than ever that hard challenges can engender truth, understanding, and self-knowledge that can push anyone to greatness," the race organizers explain.

Urbina decided to use his route as the basis for an annual mountain bike race. He called it La Ruta de Los Conquistadores in honor of those first explorers.

Is it physically and mentally testing? You bet. Perhaps not as testing as it was in the sixteenth century but, as the organizers warn, it's no amble through the park.

"As the route snakes through tropical rain forest, 12,000-ft volcanoes, banana plantations, and tiny farm towns, it alternatively drenches you in rain and freezes you in high elevation. Over every imaginable riding surface—singletrack and fireroad trails, gravel, hard-packed dirt, pavement, thigh-deep mud, sand, volcano ash, and more—the route will have you making endless granny-gear chugs, hike-a-bikes, and white-knuckle descents through and over rainforests, sweltering jungle, steaming volcanoes, breezy coastline, suspended bridges, and deep river gorges."

It sounds amazing. But it comes with no uncertain admonition. "Be forewarned," the organizers state of the 161-mile (280-km),

three-day stage race that crosses five mountain ranges and involves a cumulative 29,000 ft (8,839 m) of climbing. "La Ruta is not a race for novice mountain bikers. Even professional riders roll their eyes in disbelief when they recount what they have done. This race is a test of everything you've got— your riding abilities, physical endurance, mental strength, and equipment durability. In this struggle of joyful adversity, you may even learn something new about yourself. That's why many who experience the grueling terrain that bedeviled the original conquistadores nearly five centuries ago often describe it not merely as a 'race', but as a personal growth journey."

Here's how 2013 competitor Chris Case wrote up his race in **VeloNews**. "La Ruta is a soul-sappingly hard, exotically wild, singular journey across laughably steep inclines, hysterically steeper descents, through jungles, plantations, villages, across ecosystems and temperate zones, over volcanoes and beaches, and terrain that you never quite imagined you could ride on a bike."

INDEX

PICTURE CREDITS

Pages 2/3 Patagonian Expedition Race © Lupispuma/ Patagonian Expedition Race; pages 4/5 Ötillö © Jakob Edholm; page 6 © Wenger Patagonian Expedition Race; pages 8/9 © Daisy Gilardini Stone/Getty Images; pages 10-13 Pikes Peak © Pikes Peak Marathon, Inc.; pages 14/15 Badwater © David McNew/Getty Images; page 16 Ironman © Marco Garcia/Getty Images; page 17 Athens to Atlanta Road Skate © Johnna Keller/Margaret Price; page 18 Catalina Channel Swim © Andrew Helwich/iStock; page 20 The Iditarod © Harold Sund/Getty Images; page 21 The Iditarod © Cultura Travel/Philip Lee Harvey/ Getty Images; pages 22-25 Yukon Arctic Ultra © Montane – Martin Hartley; page 26 The Tevis Cup © Bill Gore Photography; Page 28 Tour Divide © Mike Kemp Images/Getty Images; page 29 Tour Divide © Ilan Shacham/Getty Images; page 30 Ultraman World Championships © G. Brad Lewis/Getty Images; page 33 Tough Mudder © Justin Setterfield/ Getty Images; page 34 Leadville Trail 100 © Jeremy Papasso/Glen Delman Photography; page 35 Leadville Trail 100 © Glen Delman Photography; page 36 Race Across America © Alexander Karelly/Lupispuma; pages 38-39 Grand to Grand Ultra © Grand to Grand Ultra; pages 40-41 6633 Ultra © Likeys; page 42 Western States 100-Mile Endurance Run © Greg Von Doersten/Getty Images; page 43 Western States 100-Mile Endurance Run © Jordan Siemens/Getty Images; page 45 Appalachian Trail © Gareth Mccormack/Getty Images; page 46 Ausable River Canoe Marathon © Mark Bialek; page 47 Yukon Quest © ventdusud/Getty Images; pages 48/49 Etape du Tour © DPPI/Eric Vargiolu; pages 50-51 The GR20 © tony740607/iStock Images; Page 52 The Ultra-Trail du Mont-Blanc © R. Tyler Gross/Getty Images; page 54 The English Channel Swim © Steve Hadfield and Michael Read; page 56 Race the Train © VisitBritain/Britain on View/Getty Images; page 57 Talisker Whisky Atlantic Challenge © Talisker Whisky Atlantic Challenge/Ben Duffy; page 59 Enduroman Arch © Enduroman Arch; pages 60/61 Vasaloppet © Vasaloppet; page 62 Red Bull X-Alps © Vitek Ludvik/Red Bull Content Pool; page 63 Red Bull X-Alps © Markus Berger/Red Bull Content Pool; pages 64/65 Red Bull X-Alps © Sebastian Marko/Red Bull Content Pool; page 66 Vendee Globe © Getty Images; pages 68-69 Patrouille des Glaciers © Philipp Nendaz/Patrouille des Glaciers; pages 70-71 Spartathlon © Spartathlon; pages 72-73 Virgin Money London Marathon © Virgin Money London Marathon; pages 74-76 Ötillö © Jakob Edholm; page 77 SUP 11-City Tour © SUP 11-City Tour; page 78 The Haute Route © Alpine Light & Structure/Getty Images; page 79 The Haute Route © Andre Schoenherr/Getty Images; page 80 L'Etape du Tour © ASO/EVA/Eric Vargiolu; page 81 Paris–Roubaix Challenge © Golazo sports; pages 82/83 Three Peaks Challenge © Lucy Johnston/Three Peaks Challenge Ltd; page 84 Tour de Force © Tour de Force; pages 86/87 Dusi Canoe Marathon © Anthony Grote/Gameplan Media; pages 88/89 Cape Epic © Sam Clark; pages 90/91 Cape Epic © Karin Schermbrucker; page 92 Mongol Derby © The Adventurists/Quentin Moreau; page 93 Mongol Derby © The Adventurists/Charles van Wyk; pages 94/95 Mongol Derby © The Adventurists/Tom Gildon; pages 96/97 Marathon des Sables © Ian Cumming/Design Pics/Getty Images; pages 98/99 Trans Atlas Marathon © Mark Gillett & www.lawrenceofmorocco.com; page 100 Great Ethiopian Run © Joern Pollex/Getty Images; page 101 Comrades Marathon © Comrades Marathon Association; pages 102/103 Yak Attack © Gaurav Man Scherchan; page 104 Great Wall Marathon © Klaus Sletting Jensen/Albatros Adventure; page 105 Great Wall Marathon © Klaus Sletting Jensen/Albatros Adventure; pages 106-107 Rickshaw Run © Adventurists; pages 108/109 Gobi March © www.4deserts.com; page 110-111 Dusi Canoe Marathon © Anthony Grote/Gameplan Media; pages 112/113 © Patagonian Expedition Race; page 114 The Dakar Rally © DPPI/E Vargiolu; page 115 The Dakar Rally © DPPI/F.Le Floch; page 116-117 Crocodile Trophy © Crocodile Trophy/Regina Stanger; page 118-119 Simpson Dessert Bike Challenge © Participants of the Simpson Desert Bike Challenge; page 120 Nullaboor Links © Nullaboor Links; page 122 The Everest Marathon © Visuals Unlimited, Inc./Tim Hauf/Getty Images; page 123 The Everest Marathon © Tim Johnson/MCT/MCT/Getty Images; page 124 The North Pole Marathon © destigter-photo/iStock Images; page 125 Lancelin Ocean Classic © Alberto Guglielmi © Getty Images; pages 126/127 Patagonian Expedition Race © Patagonian Expedition Race; page 128 Patagonian Expedition Race © Patagonian Expedition Race/Lupispuma; page 129 Patagonian Expedition Race © Patagonian Expedition Race/Radcliffe; page 130 Jungle Marathon © Alexander Beer; page 133 Speight's Coast to Coast © Speight's Coast to Coast; pages 134/135 Inca Trail Marathon © Andes Adventures; pages 136-137 Atacama Crossing © www.4deserts.com; pages 138-140 La Ruta de los Conquistadores © La Ruta de los Conquistadores

ACKNOWLEDGMENTS

Thanks to all the race organizers and competitors who helped with this book. And full respect to anyone who took part in any of these events. Where quotations have been used, every attempt has been made to contact the relevant competitor.

The publisher would also like to thank all the events and organisations who took the time to help out with the book, whether supplying images or offering to provide information about the races.